VOCAL
POWER

BORN TO SING

COMPLETE VOICE TRAINING

by

ELISABETH HOWARD & HOWARD AUSTIN

Inquiries should be addressed to:

VOCAL POWER
18653 Ventura Blvd. suite #551
Tarzana, CA 91356

Printed in the United States of America
First edition

Cover design by Howard Austin
Cartoon illustrations by Mike Toth
Musical illustrations by Peggy Oquist

ISBN 0-934419-00-0

*** Preface ***

One of the precious gifts of human life is the musical instrument within us......We take great pleasure in sharing with you the Method that will enable you to bring forth *your gift of singing.* With love and care, using this method, you can transform your voice.

This course IS NOT about anatomy or physiology....It IS a PRACTICAL approach, applicable to all vocal styles, from Pop to Classical, Rock'N'Roll to Opera...designed to get Results!

DISCOVER and EXPLORE:

    1)...the physical sensations and sounds of natural, healthy singing...

    2)...style and the art of expressive communication...

    3)...your individual style and sound...

    4)...basic musical skills for faster learning and better understanding of your song material...

    5)...practical knowledge for communicating with other musicians...

Have fun and keep singing,

Love, Liz & Howard

TABLE OF CONTENTS:

PART I * Technique

PART II * Style

PART III *
Sight—Singing
Ear Training

4 Cassette Course*
(with demonstrations & accompaniments)
Contents

Vol I: BASIC TECHNIQUES — Side A:
* BREATHING: intake of air, exercises..*
SUPPORT: 'out & down', feeling and using it
in all areas of the range, exercises...
* FOCUSING the vocal cords: controlling
breathiness, exercises...* VOWELS: special
attention to the 'ee' and 'oo', exercises...* UPPER REGISTER/FALSETTO: smooth
voice movement, head and chest voices, exercises...* CONSONANTS: voiced and unvoiced; staying focused; various vowels;
head and chest voice, exercises...* VOLUME
CONTROL (dynamics): chest and head voice,
exercises...

Side B:
* VOLUME CONTROL: decrescendo, crescendo,
exercises...* VIBRATO: for expressive singing; 'vocal cord'/'throat'/'diaphragmatic'
(abdominal), controlling the speed, width
and smoothness; the 'straight tone', the
delayed vibrato, exercises; chest and head
voice, more exercises...* DIPTHONGS (double
vowels): staying in the open vowel, exercises.........* PLACEMENT/RESONANCE (vocal
colors): head, nasal, mouth, chest; various
areas of the range, exercises...

*See p. 125

Vol II: ADVANCED TECHNIQUES – Side A:

SUSTAINING, DYNAMICS, RESONANCES, VIB-
RATO – APPLIED: to song phrases, exercises
...* BREATHINESS: for expressive singing;
sustaining with control, exercises.........
CRESCENDO and DECRESCENDO, (smooth VOLUME
change), exercises.....* VIBRATO: control,
intensity, * VARIATIONS & COMBINATIONS for
MOOD PAINTING APPLIED to song phrases;
blending with other voices......* SPECIAL
EFFECTS: using volume, resonance & vibrato,
plus combinations...

Side B:

Throat VIBRATO: special effects, exercises
.....* REGISTER BREAK: blending, * UPPER
MIXTURE: exercises; applied to song phrases
* IMPROVISATION, PHRASING, "LICKS": vocal
agility and flexibility; exercises........
* PERSONAL STYLE: special effects, song
phrases; exercises...* UPPER REGISTER (HEAD
VOICE, FALSETTO, SOPRANO): comparing "Pop"
sound with "Legit" (classical sound); exercises, variations...* CLASSICAL TECHNIQUES:
vibrato – placement – resonance – colors;
exercises; lower mixed register; exercises;
Staccato, exercises; Trill, exercises...

Vol III: STYLE – Side A:

Do It With STYLE: style components * BLUES:
scale, exercises; influencing the melody,
song phrases – Blues/Country – Blues/Rock;
* IMPROVISING: added and hidden notes.....
* "LICKS" * RHYTHM & BLUES/SOUL * ROCK em-
bellishments.....* CLASSICAL improvisation
(coloratura); TRILL (half step and whole
step), exercises; STACCATO, exercises......
CADENZA, exercises...

Vol III — Side B:
ROCK: Pentatonic scale, song phrases, exercises.....* VERSATILITY: pronunciation —
vibrato — voice coloring — phrasing applied
to Country, R & B, Rock; song phrases,
exercises....* BROADWAY: character voices;
vibrato...* PHRASING: expressiveness, song
phrases, exercises; how to build emotional
intensity, exercises...

Vol IV: VOCAL EXERCISES — Side A:
WORK-OUT, WARM-UP: for perfecting your
control of focus — vibrato — dynamics —
resonance and range, etc......use once or
more daily...

Side B — EAR TRAINING EXERCISES:
Sharpen your sense of pitch and harmony;
Major scale — octave — intervals — Major
triad — Major seventh; minor scale —
intervals — minor triad — minor seventh;
Dominant seventh...* BLUES scale, improvisation, more EXERCISES: scales — intervals
— chords; Blues...

✳ Acknowledgments ✳

To those who *Inspired*, *Shared* and *Supported*
the singing and music in our lives...

thank you

* John DeMain * John Motley * Dr. Peter J.
Wilhousky & the boys & girls of the All
City Chorus, NYC * Mike Scott-'mon bon' *
Sydney Schulsinger, dad * Lillian Seinberg
* James Levine * Ben Chancey * Al Hibbler *
* Geoffrey G. Forward- ♥ * Gloria Lane *
Samuel Krachmalnick * Philip Lanza Sandor *
Gluck Sandor * David Gottlieb * Joanna
Lanza * Pauline Domanski * Rosalie Bradd *
Julia and Hans Heinz * Joseph Papp * Sam
Brown, III * Edith DelValle * George Saslow
* Abba Bogin * Rose Busen Corigliano *
Vittorio Giannini * Arnold Fish * Sergius
Kagen * Madeleine Marshall * Gunter Stern *
Alton Jones * Martha Levitsky * Michael
Costanza * Mme. Marion Freschl * Carlo
Moresco * Martin Rich * Eleanor Steber *
Curt Allen * Christina Pickard * David
'Cat' Cohen * Dean Wilford Bain * Virginia
MacWaters * Steven Williams * Barbara Gamm
Frenkel * Fern Newman * George Ogee * Fred
Feldt * Belle- mom * Nina Lanza Wayne-mom *
Judy Lamppu * Joseph Pandolfini-dad I *
Sabino Infante-dad II * Joey Forward * N.G.
Levine & the boys & girls of Midwood High
Chorus * Mario Lanza * Roberta Peters *
Dietrich Fischer-Diskau * Robert Goulet *
Judy Garland * J.S. Bach * W.A. Mozart *

Special thanks to Geoffrey G. Forward for
contributing his editorial and literary ex-
pertise to the fulfillment of this project.

Excerpt from GREAT SINGERS ON GREAT SINGING
by Jerome Hines, Copyright © 1982 by
Jerome Hines; Reprinted by permission of
Doubleday & company, Inc..

✷ Breathing ✷

The voice is a wind instrument and you need breath to play it. For singing, unlike speaking or relaxed breathing, filling the lungs completely is important. Obviously, the more breath you take, the longer phrase you can sing. What is not so obvious is that a full breath tends to give you better vocal control for high notes, low notes, soft, loud, tone coloring, flexibility for 'licks', vibrato, straight tone (non-vibrato), clear tone, singing smoothly through the registers, etc..

Intake Of Air

The intake of air through the open mouth and nose is recommended. Inhaling through the nose alone is not preferred for the following reasons:

    1. You cannot obtain as deep and quick a breath through the nose as you can through the <u>mouth and nose</u> since the nasal passage alone presents greater resistance to the air intake.

    2. The nose breath is usually facially unattractive and distracts from the performance.

3. If you have a cold, it is much more difficult or even impossible to breathe through the nose...and trying to do so may create undesirable sounds.

Breathing through the nose is more acceptable when there is adequate time to breathe, such as during the instrumental introduction to a song or during an interlude ('break'). Even then, the mouth breath is still preferred for the above reasons.

Try to time your breath so that you don't "hold" your air before you sing. Holding the air tends to tighten the throat muscles. If you do get into a situation where you have taken a breath too early, hold it with a relaxed, open throat by sustaining a comfortable expansion of the rib cage and lower stomach.

Rib Cage & Lower Stomach

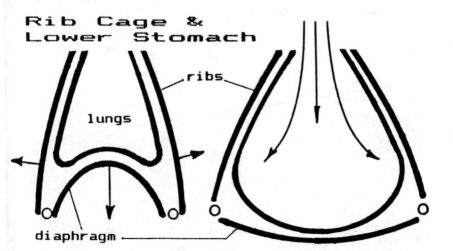

The rib cage encases or surrounds the lungs. It is expandable and **must** expand for the intake of air. The singer must help the rib cage open in order to draw in the air through the open mouth and nose. This principle applies to the lower stomach as well. The diaphragmatic muscle must move down, opening up additional space while the lower stomach relaxes and expands with the intake of air, like expanding out against a belt around your waist as you inhale. The objective here is to make room for the lungs to inflate to their fullest capacity by allowing them to expand downward as well outward.

Guidelines:

1. The intake of air should appear natural and effortless. You don't want your audience to be distracted or feel uncomfortable. You don't want them to breathe with you or even be aware of your breathing.

2. The upper chest and shoulders should remain relaxed when taking a breath. Raising them can cause undesirable tensions in the upper body and throat.

3. Don't pull the stomach in or up since this action inhibits the expansion of the lungs.

EXERCISES:

1. Place your open hands on your hips and slide them upward about three inches until your thumbs reach the lower ribs towards the back. Now, take a full breath through a comfortably open mouth, nose and throat, expanding your ribs outward against your thumbs and hands, pushing them apart. Allow the lower stomach to expand at the same time. The shoulders do not rise but remain relaxed

and down. Relax your neck and jaw. Feel
your tongue forward and relaxed, resting
the tip against the lower teeth. Feel a
kind of yawning sensation that lets the
incoming air cool the back of your
throat.

Inhale (✓) for 2 seconds and hiss out
for 4 seconds, 3 times in a row.

    IN, 2 -- OUT, 2, 3, 4
     (✓)   (ssssssssssss)

    IN, 2 -- OUT, 2, 3, 4
     (✓)   (ssssssssssss)

    IN, 2 -- OUT, 2, 3, 4
     (✓)   (ssssssssssss)

Singing and swimming are similar in this
respect...The longer the swimmer exhales in
the water, the more air he or she must take
in on the next breath. For the singer, the
longer the phrase, the more air he or she
must take in on the next breath. Always
begin with a full, deep breath, replen-
ishing the air between phrases.

NOTE: In order to obtain fresh oxygen and
to relax the respiratory system, it is
advisable, when time permits between
phrases, to exhale more completely.

    2.   After a full breath, using the teeth
    as resistance to the air pressure, hiss
    out for 4 counts. Replenish the air in 1
    count. Hiss out for 5 counts. Take a
    full breath in 1 count. Hiss out for 6
    counts. Replenish in 1 count...and so
    on, increasing the duration of the hiss
    to at least 10 or 15 counts, always
    replenishing the air in 1 count.

Keep the air pressure steady throughout
the hiss. Don't pause between taking in
air and using the air. Keep the breath
flowing. This exercise will help train
you to breathe quickly and deeply allowing you to extend the length of your
song phrase.

✳ Support ✳

The "out and down" approach to support that
we are about to discuss will give you the
most precise control of air pressure. It
will also give you access to POWER which
must be used within appropriate limits in
order to keep your voice healthy.

The number one <u>killer</u> of the voice is
"pushing" air too forcefully through the
vocal cords forcing them open and/or causing the throat to squeeze. The exhaling
muscles are capable of forcing air too hard
for the vocal cords to withstand. Pushing
is most likely to occur when singing high
and/or loud.

Pushing will irritate the vocal cords, resulting in a tired, hoarse voice. Irritated
tissues are more susceptible to infection.
If this kind of abuse is repeated and
prolonged, it could lead to more permanent
vocal disability; the formation of callous-
like tissue or "nodules" (nodes) on the
vocal cords. This condition may require a
surgical procedure to correct as well as
extended vocal rest. We cannot replace the
vocal cords as we can replace the reeds of
other wind instruments. The voice needs
rest and time to recuperate from stress
....and the singer must adjust his or her
vocal technique.

OUT AND DOWN SUPPORT: The singer, like the

wind instrument player, uses air pressure
to create tone. We control air pressure
with the same muscles we use for coughing,
sneezing and laughing. Luciano Pavarotti,
in "Great Singers On Great Singing" by
Jerome Hines, says, "*like a woman in labor,
giving birth*" also "*as when you're in the
bathroom and you keep this position until
the phrase is finished*". We often refer to
this as the 'out and down' support because
that is a good description of the physical
sensation we experience. This approach will
give you <u>precision control of air pressure</u>,
an essential element in voice control.

EXERCISES:

1. Place your finger tips or your
thumbs firmly against the soft area at
your sides, below your lowest rib and
above your hip bone. Now, cough gently 2
times. That outward pressure you feel
against your finger tips is natural support. Feel it again, using a loud hiss.
Now, on 'F', as in 'fame' (fff,fff). Make
sure you feel the same gentle but firm
outward pressure against your finger
tips.

2. Now, feel your support working
behind a vocal tone. Use 2 strong hisses
followed by an easy, 'shout-like' sound.
Breathe (✓) after the 2 hisses and
before the 'shout':

(✓)sss,sss(✓)hey!

The support you feel with the hisses begins
when the hiss begins. But for singing,
<u>establish the support just prior to and
maintain it to the end of the vocal sound</u>.
Feel the same easy 'out and down' support
on the 'shout' as on the hisses.

3.   Repeat three times....

(✓)sss,sss(✓)hey!
(✓)sss,sss(✓)hey!
(✓)sss,sss(✓)hey!

4.   Do the same thing with a longer
tone at the end like this:

(✓)sss,sss(✓)heeeeeeeeey.

5.   Try it in various parts of your
vocal range; low, middle and high. Repeat this exercise with various other
vowels sounds after the hisses:

sss,sss(✓)aaaaaaaaa (as in 'hat')
sss,sss(✓)ooooooooo (as in 'you')
sss,sss(✓)aaaaaaaah (as in 'hot')
sss,sss(✓)eeeeeeeee (as in 'he')
sss,sss(✓)uuuuuuuuh (as in 'hum')
sss,sss(✓)aaaaaaaaw (as in 'awning)
etc.

There is a tendency to relax support as air
pressure decreases for soft volume or low
notes. But support should remain constant
during any vocal production.

6.   Check support with your
     finger tips and hiss:
loud:
    (✓) (support----------)
        sssssssssssssssss
soft:
    (✓) (support----------)
        sssssssssssssssss

Notice that support tends to relax when air
pressure is low but don't let it.

7. Alternate several times until
you are able to establish the same firm

support for the soft as for the loud.

    8.   Start   with   a   loud   hiss   and smoothly   decrescendo   without   relaxing support. Use your finger tips to check.

  (✓) (support--------------)
      ssssssssssssssssssss
    (══════════════════)

HELPFUL SUGGESTIONS
FOR THE TIRED VOICE

    1. If your voice is   tired   or   hoarse, rest it totally. Do <u>not</u> sing, talk or   even whisper.   If you must rehearse, just 'mark' your music.   That is, go through the   piece for tempo, dynamics,   arrangement,   general feel, etc..   If you choose to   sing,   don't sing louder than half   voice   (mezzo   voce) with as clear a tone as possible.   <u>A   won-derfully performed rehearsal is not worth a bad performance..or no performance at all!</u>

    2. Warm   beverages   soothe   the   throat area. Avoid drinking piping hot liquids.

    3.   Gargling with warm salt water or   a strong mouthwash   (menthol/eucalyptus)   may also be helpful.

    4. Breathing vapors containing   menthol or eucalyptus is very soothing.

    5. When singing with a band, be sure to have an adequate monitoring system for   the voice.   A   small   speaker   or   two,   facing towards you as you sing, allows you to hear yourself. When you can't hear yourself, you tend to think you can't be heard above   the amplified sound of the   band   and   you   may 'push'. Learn to *feel* your voice.

      ✳   ✳   ✳   ✳   ✳   ✳

* Focusing *
* The Vocal Cords *

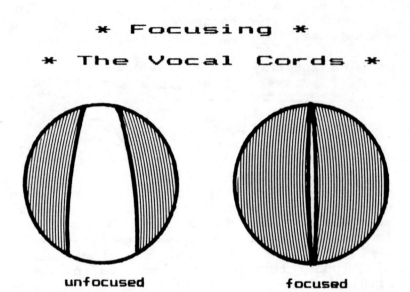

unfocused   focused

When air passes through vocal cords that
are 'focused' or approximating, the vocal
cords vibrate, producing vocal sound. When
focused, the vocal cords may be imagined as
a skin stretched across a drum and slit
down the center. When unfocused, the vocal
cords are too open (above), allowing too
much air through, resulting in a breathy
and sometimes raspy tone. This can cause
friction, irritating the vocal cord tissue.
You may even feel a tickle which could
evoke a coughing reaction.

Prolonged breathy or raspy singing can
cause the build-up of excessive mucus which
is the body's mechanism for protecting the
vocal cords. Remember, when singing high
and loud, don't push the air so hard that
you unfocus your voice. Breathiness or a
raspy sound, in some isolated moments, is

actually desirable for emotional emphasis. However, because more air must be used to produce the unfocused tones, it is more difficult to sing long sustained musical phrases. This is why some singers are constantly <u>out of breath</u> at the end of their phrases. Singing breathy can be exhausting and detract from the energy level of the performance.

If you *focus*, you will be able to sustain tones, reduce throat problems and expand your range and flexibility.

FORWARD PLACEMENT
MASK RESONANCE

Forward placement/'mask' resonance: the result of the focused tone resonating through a clear channel; a sense of the vocal sound resonating against the bony surfaces around the nose, including the bridge of the nose and the upper front teeth (see nasal, mouth resonances, pp. 14 & 39-42). Let's locate the vocal cords and develop control of focusing the tone through the mask resonance.

EXERCISES:

　　　1. With your mouth open, <u>as if ready</u> <u>to bite an apple</u>, in a gentle but firm scolding tone, say "aa...aa...aa..." (as in "hat").

Try not to 'cough' out the tone. Listen and feel the 'buzzing' sound of the focused tone (not breathy). Feel your support and P use your finger tips to check.

2. Now sustain the last "aa", like this:

"aa...aa...aaaaaaaaaaaaa"

Maintain that energetic and buzzing sound as you sustain the vowel.

3. Using other vowels at the end, try to match the energy that you feel on "aaaaaaaaaa" in the other vowels that follow it:

"aa...aa...aaaaaaaaa (as in 'hat')
"aa...aa...ooooooooh (as in 'home')
"aa...aa...eeeeeeeee (as in 'he')
"aa...aa...aaaaaaaah (as in 'far')
"aa...aa...uuuuuuuuh (as in 'hum')
"aa...aa...oooooooooo (as in 'who')
 etc...

❋   ❋   ❋   ❋   ❋   ❋

* Vowels *

Articulation

The vowel sounds are formed by shaping the mouth space, using the <u>tongue</u>, <u>lips</u> and <u>jaw</u>. The tip of the tongue should rest behind the lower teeth on all the vowel sounds, moving only to articulate consonants and quickly returning to its resting place. If the tongue pulls back, it blocks the throat passage, interfering with resonance and possibly with focus as well.

In the following progression, the tongue lowers from its highest position for "ee" to its lowest position for "oo" with the tip resting behind the lower teeth. For the "aw", "uu" and "oo", the lips, in addition to the tongue, are involved; further forward for each sound and most rounded for "oo".

```
      "ee" as in 'he'
      "ih" as in 'him'
      "eh" as in 'hen'
      "aa" as in 'hat'
    * "ah" as in 'far'
      "aw" as in 'ought'
      "uu" as in 'hook'
      "oo" as in 'who'
```

"ah" as in the bright Boston vowel

High and/or loud tones need room in order to sound free and easy. The vowels, therefore, open up and become slightly modified accordingly. The shape of the mouth should widen towards the smile but <u>never</u> become a grimace or unnatural in appearance. For example, if the expression of a word indicates sorrow, the eyes are the source of that communication and the mouth still widens, especially on higher and/or louder tones. Notice that in both crying and smiling, the expression of the mouth is quite similar.

Let the eye teeth show slightly and be careful not to wrinkle the nose or tense the lips unnaturally. The widened mouth position helps to activate the mask resonance, adding overtones that give the voice richness throughout its range. This is particularly effective when you are singing a song in which the range seems too low. Brighten your vowel sounds by widening the mouth position horizontally, as in the smile, which emphasizes your upper resonances along with the chest color.

For the vowels:
> "ee" as in 'he',
> "ih" as in 'him' and
> "oo" as in 'who'

there is a tendency to close the jaw and throat space.

The tongue creates the "ee" sound (as in 'he'), with the edges of the middle tongue touching the upper molars on both sides of the mouth, with the tip resting behind the lower teeth.

When the "ee" vowel occurs on a high note, it is best to lower the position slightly as in the sound "ih" (as in 'him') while the jaw opens a little bit more in order to produce a free and open vowel. You should try, nevertheless, to maintain as pure an "ee" vowel as possible. This method applies to louder tones as well, especially if the chest resonance is emphasized (see

p. 45).

The lips create the "oo" sound and, as in the case of "ee", it is best to lower (not force) the jaw open for higher and/or louder tones. The mouth must open further than it normally would for the pure "oo" in the speaking voice range. Even when the jaw is more open, try to maintain the pure "oo" by reaching with the lips to form a round shape. It may feel a little awkward at first to form the "oo" sound with the jaw more open than it is for speech; however, the result is an unblocked, rich vocal quality.

EXERCISES:

1. Open your mouth about an inch and a half and press your finger tips against your cheeks so that you can feel your open teeth inside and say,

(as in 'hot') "ah...ah...eeeeeeeee".

Notice the tendency to close the jaw on the "ee" vowel.

2. Now, do it again, keeping the open space you feel on the "ah" vowel right through the "ee" vowel. Allow the tongue to make the "ee" with the tip resting behind the lower teeth.

3. Do the same thing for both the "ih" and the "oo" vowels.

"ah...ah...iiiiiiiih"
"ah...ah...oooooooooo"

DIPTHONGS (double vowels — see p. 34)

‗   ‗   ‗   ‗   ‗   ‗   ‗

✳ Consonants ✳

Consonants are speech sounds that interupt
the free flow of vocal tone. If you let
them, they can get in the way by interfering with the focus of the vocal cords
and the freedom of the open space (throat,
mouth and nasal areas).

VOICED & UNVOICED CONSONANTS

The voiced consonants are those in which
the vocal cords vibrate, creating vocal
sound. Unvoiced or aspirated consonants are
those in which the vocal cords are open and
do not vibrate.

Below are pairs of voiced and unvoiced consonants, matched with respect to the position of the articulators (mouth, lips, jaw,
tongue, teeth, hard palate, soft palate).

HARD PALATE: roof of the mouth.

SOFT PALATE: soft area behind
the hard palate, at the back of
the roof of the mouth.

The following is a partial list of these
consonant pairs:

VOICED   UNVOICED

b (as in 'bay')....p (as in 'pay')

d (as in 'do').....t (as in 'too')

g (as in 'glue')...k (as in 'clue')

g (as in 'gem ')....ch('chat')

th(as in 'the')....th(as in 'thanks')

v (as in 'van')....f (as in 'fan')

z (as in 'zoo')....s (as in 'Sue')

OTHER VOICED CONSONANTS:

l (as in 'line')
m (as in 'more')
n (as in 'now')
r (as in 'reel')

Consonants may also appear in combination.
For example:

bz(as in 'tabs')...ps(as in 'taps')
dz(as in 'woods)...ts(as in 'cats')
gz(as in 'fogs')...ks(as in 'folks')

'SILENT H'

'H' is a special case of unvoiced consonant
since it does not require the action of the
articulators. The 'silent H' can helps you
avoid a GLOTTAL ATTACK (see p. 23)

Place your finger tips at the front of your throat and say, "zzzzzzzzzzz", with a strong buzzing sound. That vibration you feel against your finger tips is from your vibrating vocal cords. The voiced consonant requires the vocal cords to focus and vibrate.

Now, say, "sssssssssss", with a good, strong hissing sound. Notice there is no vibration against your finger tips. The unvoiced consonant requires the vocal cords to open and, therefore, not vibrate.

Since the vocal cords must open for the unvoiced consonants, there tends to be a delayed and/or diminished focus in the vowel that follows. A good way to counteract this tendency is to reduce the duration of the unvoiced consonant by <u>thinking</u> the voiced consonant counterpart (refer to the above pairs). This helps focus take place immediately following the consonant. It is best to 'think' the focused vowel that follows the consonant.

EXERCISES:

   1.   Using the above pairs of voiced and unvoiced consonants, speak or sing:

   bay...pay...bay...pay...

Continue down the list.

   2.   Place your finger tips at the front of your throat and say "zzzzzzzz" with a strong buzzing sound. That vibration you feel against your finger tips is from your vibrating vocal cords.

Now, say "ssssss" with a good strong hissing sound. Notice that there is no vibration against your finger tips.

3. You can feel the vocal cords alternately open and focus in the following exercise. Keep a steady flow of air as you alternate between "ZZZZZZZ" (voiced) and "SSSSSSS" (unvoiced):

(✓)zzzzzsssssszzzzzsssssszzzzzsssss
and:
(✓)vvvvvffffffvvvvvffffffvvvvvffffff

Both consonants in each pair require the same position of the tongue, teeth, jaw and lips. But the unvoiced consonant, "sss" and "fffff", require the vocal cords to be open (unfocused). With your finger tips at your throat, say "the zoo" and then say "the suit".

Notice the interruption of focus during the "sss" in the word 'suit'....a gap in the stream of vocal tone.

Reduce the forcefulness of the consonants without losing clarity. Think the focused vowel that follows the consonant even before you pronounce the consonant.

4. In the following exercise, match the focus of the "aaa" (as in hat) in the vowel of the word that follows it. Don't let the consonant introduce excessive breath into the vocal tone.

aaa...aaa...haaat
aaa...aaa...saaad
aaa...aaa...caaatch
aaa...aaa...scaaat

```
aaa...aaa...chaaat
aaa...aaa...faaast
aaa...aaa...shaaack
aaa...aaa...staaack
```

Use the same principle with a variety of words, like those contained in the list on page 7.

Example:

"ee...ee...he", "ih...ih...him", etc.

When moving from a vowel to a consonant, do not anticipate the consonant by shortening the sustained vowel and don't alter the vowel as you approach the consonant. Closing too early toward the consonant shape tends to interfere with focus and resonating space.

* Volume Control *

Dynamics

To be an exciting and versatile vocal artist, you must be able to control dynamics;
soft, loud and all the shades between;
crescendo, decrescendo; sing full, rich
tones as well as the soft, intimate tones
...and all the possible variations.

<u>To sing with greater volume</u> or to crescendo
(<u>   </u> , softer to louder), increase
air pressure and hold the focused vocal
cord position more firmly.

For the fullest and loudest tones, also
increase resonating space to the maximum
(see "Placement, Resonance, Vocal Colors",
p. 39). But, be careful not to 'push'! When
the air pressure is perfectly balanced
against the focusing vocal cords in open
resonators, you will experience a "buzzing"
sound or 'ring' in your voice.

<u>For singing softer tones</u> or decrescendo
(<u>   </u> , louder to softer), decrease
air pressure and focusing strength. For the
softest tones, a yawn-like sensation will
help you relax the focusing strength,
allowing the delicate fringes of the vocal
cords to vibrate. Be careful to maintain
firm, steady, <u>out and down</u> support.

EXERCISES:

1. On "nyaaaah" ('a' as in 'at'), use a siren-like slide, within a comfortable vocal range and slide your voice slowly up and down with fairly full volume. Keep the volume and vowel constant throughout, maintaining the cords in the focused position for a clear tone.

On the downward part of the slide, be careful not to relax support. Use your finger tips to check. The jaw should gradually open wider for the higher range and return to a slightly less open position for the lower range. Maintain a continuous focus throughout the slide without breathy interruptions of the tone quality.

Do not hold the cords so tightly that your throat squeezes and air has to be 'pushed' through. You will lose the buzz and resonant ring in the tone and you may irritate your voice.

2. Repeat this <u>siren</u> exercise with medium volume and again at low volume.

<u>Balance is the key to vocal control.</u> Although the cords relax to balance the decreased air pressure for softer volume, they must produce a clear tone throughout and the vowel must be kept pure and open. Note that the 'buzz' is not as noticeable when singing softer. When using the yawn to help relax the focusing strength, you may feel as though you are opening the

cords even though they are still focusing.

　　　3. Now, use the siren with other vowel sounds: "eh", "oh", "ee" and "oo".

　　　4. Sing:

A.	LOUD	SOFT	LOUD	mmmm
B.	SOFT	LOUD	SOFT	mmmm
C.	SOFT	MEDIUM	LOUD	mmmm
D.	LOUD	MEDIUM	SOFT	mmmm

Crescendo and decrescendo are basic to expressive singing. Use a variety of vowels ...Be creative!

'SILENT H':

A slight, <u>inaudible</u> "H" at the beginning of a syllable will help prevent an audible "glottal" attack. The cords should draw together (lightly for the softest tones) rather than beginning in a closed position and popping open, as in a cough. 'Think' the "H"; don't sound it. Feel the open passage for that sound.

Big Voice/small voice

When the voice is expected to project without electronic amplification, as in opera and oratorio, the inherent size and quality ('timbre', color) of the voice is a significant factor. But in pop music, the voice is almost always amplified. The singer depends more on individual style and emotional intensity.

There are areas of classical repertoire, such as chamber music, Lieder (art songs), oratorio (church and choral), where vocal size is not as important as artistry. There are some singers who perform in all areas of classical music, from opera to chamber music and other singers who specialize, either by choice or because of their inherent vocal size. Even within the operatic repertoire, there are singers who sing only the lighter operas (e.g., Mozart, Rossini) as compared to the more dramatic works (e.g., Verdi, Wagner).

While your voice is maturing, you should avoid the heavier, more dramatic roles. Some singers are overambitious, unaware or ill-advised and work on roles beyond their endurance. A singer may *feel* the music of a particular composer but unfortunately, must limit the repertoire to works more suitable to the inherent size of the voice.

* Vibrato *

Expressive singing

Professional singers, with few exceptions, in most areas of vocal music, use vibrato for expressive singing. It is a popular misconception that vibrato is used only by opera singers. If your career is to include studio work, back-up or group singing, the ability to control your vibrato and 'straight tone' (tone without vibrato) is a <u>basic requirement</u>.

Vibrato is a pulse or wave in a sustained tone. It gives the voice a polished and professional sound. The ability to control your vibrato as you hold a note is extremely important, for any vocal style.

Vibrato is rarely explored in depth in voice training, although it is one of the primary objectives in the study of string instruments and most wind instruments.

A string player, such as a violinist or guitarist, creates the vibrato by pressing down on the string with the finger in a rapid back and forth motion. This motion causes the string to lengthen and shorten alternately, producing a slight fluctuation in pitch. A quicker back and forth motion produces a faster vibrato and a slower motion produces a slower vibrato. The player may control the vibrato speed and where to use it, according to his or her artistic taste.

A wind player, such as a flutist or clarinetist, produces vibrato by fluctuating the air pressure, sending it through the instrument in a pulsing or wave-like motion. This may be controlled with the lips, throat and/or abdominal muscles.

The following quotes show an amusing variety of misinformation and lack of clear knowledge even among *professionals*:

   "*..only opera singers need vibrato..*"

   "*It's a gift from God.*"

   "*Vibrato is not pure. It distorts the sound of beautiful resonance.*"

   "*..I plant the seed in your subconscious...every lesson, I water the seed.*"

   "*Vibrato is an undesirable effect because it causes a tremolo.*"

   "*It's an emotional reaction when you're excited about the song.*"

   "*Rock singers don't need vibrato.*"

   "*You can't teach vibrato.*"

Even the Harvard Dictionary of Music states that, among singers, there is "*uncertainty as to what vibrato means*" and refers to the "*singer's use of it without being aware of doing so.*"

VIBRATO FOR THE SINGER:

Vocal vibrato is the slight fluctuation of pitch and volume in a sustained tone. In general, the pitch variation should be minimized to an interval, spanning about a quarter tone. (A quarter tone is half the span of the half step interval.) If this interval is exceeded, the tone might sound 'wobbly' or off-pitch or disturbing to the listener. It's rare but there are singers who use a wide vibrato effectively, sometimes even as wide as a minor 3rd (e.g., C-A-C-A-C-A).

The average vibrato rate is 5 to 9 pulses per second.

Essentially, we can identify three types of vocal vibrato:

"Diaphragmatic" (Abdominal) Vibrato

The diaphragmatic vibrato is produced by pulsations activated by the abdominal muscles, while supporting steadily. The pulses cause the air to flow through the vocal cords in a wave-like motion, creating a slight fluctuation in pitch and volume. Using this method, you can control the speed and/or width (pitch variation) of your vibrato. With diaphragmatic vibrato, you experience "singing on the breath"......... a free-flowing vocal tone.

"Vocal Cord Vibrato"

Vocal cord vibrato is achieved by producing rapid interruptions in the focus of the vocal cords. This vibrato has a kind of "machine gun" quality, something like the "ba-aa-aa" of a lamb or a rapid laugh. Its versatility is limited with respect to speed and width. Vocal cord vibrato is typical of the singing styles of certain cultures (e.g., Mid-East). It is a familiar quality of the French "chanteuse" (cabaret singer) and common among American folk singers.

"Throat Vibrato"

Throat vibrato is a common type of vibrato, produced by the fluctuation of the throat muscles around the vocal cords (raising and lowering the larynx). The throat vibrato is usually slower and wider than the vocal cord vibrato and is a little more versatile with respect to speed and width. Some singers use this technique either exclusively or in combination with the diaphragmatic vibrato. It is common, probably because people tend to think of the voice as located in the throat and use throat muscles to try to imitate the sounds of the professional singers they listen to, even though those singers may not be using throat vibrato. Many jazz singers use it to imitate instrumental style.

The type of vibrato used depends on the musical material and is, ultimately, an artistic choice. However, we recommend abdominal vibrato for the following reasons:

1. Smooth diaphragmatic vibrato guarantees good, steady support because it requires that kind of support to work well.

2. Since throat muscles do not participate directly in the production of the abdominal vibrato, there is less danger of undesirable tension in the throat area which may cause shaking of the tongue, jaw and/or head.

3. When using the abdominal vibrato, the throat can remain relaxed and open which allows a deeper and richer tone quality or resonance.

4. Since the throat vibrato uses muscular pressure in the throat area, there is a greater tendency to fluctuate pitch and to flat on sustained tones. Use throat vibrato with discretion!

Some singers have styles that are recognizable by the uniqueness of their vibrato; it can even be their trademark. But surprisingly few singers are aware of how they produce their vibrato. Many teachers and singers alike claim that the vibrato is "natural". However, no one is born with a vibrato. If not learned from a teacher, it is commonly learned through imitating other singers.

It is to every singer's advantage to notice the various types of vibrato used by artists in all areas of vocal music. For example, R&B (Rhythm & Blues) singers, in general, use a slower vibrato than opera singers. Jazz singers imitate the many instrumental vibrato styles of the trumpet, sax, etc.. Pop singers, in general use vibrato more sparingly than classical singers, often beginning a sustained tone with no vibrato ('straight' tone), leading into the vibrato.

The vibrato speed may vary from one song to another and also within a song, changing with the emotional dynamics. Usually, a slower vibrato is used in a slower song and a faster vibrato in a faster song. Speeding up the vibrato as you sustain a tone increases the energy and intensity of the sound. Your voice is an amazingly versatile instrument, so become aware of the various possibilities and explore your options.

THE STRAIGHT TONE

The study of vibrato and its uses is in-complete without considering the 'straight tone'. The straight tone is a sustained note without vibrato. It is also an inte-gral part of vocal expression and emotional coloration. Moving melodic lines of quarter notes or shorter duration are almost always straight tones.

In Pop music, a sustained note usually be-gins with a straight tone moving gradually into the vibrato.

(———∿∿∿)

Very rarely, if ever, would a tone begin as a fast vibrato, slowing down to a straight tone. This effect is not standard but it is conceivable since anything is possible in the realm of artistic interpretation.

In classical style, the straight tone is used in early music, such as the Gregorian chant and music of the Renaissance; by late Romantic com-posers, like Richard Strauss and Richard Wagner; and by many composers of the 20th Century such as Alban Berg, Anton Webern and Arnold Schonberg.

Exercises for
Diaphragmatic Vibrato

1. Using the exclamation, "Hey!", send out an easy 'shout-like' sound, as if calling to someone across a crowded room. The out and down sensation of the support mechanism along with <u>good focus and forward placement</u> is the balance to strive for. Don't push!

2. Without stopping the tone send out a "Hey!" with 2 pulses:

He-ey! (not "Hey!-hey!")

You should feel subtle pulses within the abdominal area as a slight but definite outward action (not up and in). Keep the pulses even — A metronome can be helpful. Keep the jaw relaxed and flexible. You can also use a "hiss" instead of the "Hey!" to practice the vibrato. Alternating between pulsing the "hiss" and pulsing the vocal sound is an effective way of developing your vibrato control.

3. Increase the number of pulses to:

s-s-s
3 pulses: & He-e-ey!

s-s-s-s-s
5 pulses: & He-e-e-e-ey!

```
              s-s-s-s-s-s-s-s-s
9 pulses:  &  He-e-e-e-e-e-e-e-ey!
```

Written out as note values, this exercise would read as follows:

HEY!   HE-E-EY!   HE-E-E-E-EY!

HE-E-E-E-E-E-E-E-EY!

    4. Repeat the same exercise using a single sustained tone. Choose a medium high pitch and a medium loud volume since it is easier to feel the resistance when air pressure and focusing strength are greater.

Don't 'bounce' the support; keep it steady for smoother vibrato control. Check with your finger tips against the abdominal area for steady support.

As you progress, try other variations... ...high, low, loud, soft.

Try not to let the pitch vary or wobble. Think of the vibrato as *ripples on the surface of a flowing stream of sound.*

    5. Using the words "now and then", sing:

NA-Ă-Ă-Ă-AW   AND   THĚ-Ĕ-Ĕ-Ĕ-ĔN   AND   *(repeat)*

Repeat this exercise, moving up a half step at a time. Vary word combinations; vary volume. Use 'practice phrases' (page 113).

    6. Using a single open vowel 'ah' or 'eh', first loud, then soft, sing:

Repeat, moving up in half steps using your 'practice phrases'. Practice both continuous and delayed vibrato.

    7. On a single open vowel, sing:

Repeat, using the 'practice phrases'.

    8. Using a slow song, isolate the words that you would like to sustain and practice these individual words using 3 or 5 or 9 or more pulses of vibrato

(depending on how long you hold the note). Be specific.

In performance, you would never count pulses, but as a practice technique, this is an excellent way of perfecting your control. A singer with diaphragmatic vibrato control can design the vibrato speed to the desired emotional energy level and create wonderful musical effects.

Work on speeding up and slowing down the vibrato rate, keeping a smooth, gradual flow with even pulses. Experiment with a sustained straight tone moving gradually into vibrato.

Don't close the throat or cords to end a sustained tone, but release the sound using the last vibrato pulse. Make it sound as though it vanished into 'thin air' and not clipped, coughed or choked off. Understand that mastering the vibrato may take time and patience, but the professional sound you achieve is well worth it.

DIPTHONGS

A dipthong is a combination vowel, actually two vowel sounds back to back:

    My...<M/ah/ee>

(ah/ee)...ah(as in 'hot') ee(as in 'he')
    Day...<D/eh/ee>

(eh/ee)...eh(as in 'hen') ee(as in 'he')
    Boy...<B/aw/ee>

(aw/ee)...aw(as in 'dawn') ih(as in 'he')
    Now...<N/aa/oo>

(aa/oo)...aa(as in 'at') oo(as in 'who')

Go...<G/aw/oo>
(aw/oo)...aw(as in 'dawn') oo(as in 'who')

NOTE: "ee" may vary toward "ih", "oo"
toward "uu" and "aa" toward "ah".

The general rule to follow when sustaining
a tone on a dipthong is to sustain the
first vowel sound and tag on the second
vowel sound and consonant (if any) on the
end of the final vibrato pulse.

(Day)......Deh − − − − − − − ehee

(Why)......Wah − − − − − − − ahee

(Now)......Naa − − − − − − − aaoo

(Boy)......Baw − − − − − − − awee

(Go).......Guh − − − − − − − uhoo

(Smiled)..Smah − − − − − − − aheeld

Watch out for the consonant "R" following a
vowel (storm, hard, etc.). There is a
tendency to close the vowel and move to the
"R" too soon. Stay on the open vowel and
save the "R" for the end of the final pulse
of vibrato:

(Hard)...Hah − − − − − − − ahrd

THROAT VIBRATO

This technique should be reserved for special effects and styling.

The simplest way to feel the sensation of
the throat vibrato is to move your voice
quickly back and forth through the interval
of the minor 3rd (e.g., A to C).

The result is a kind of wobble. Now, decrease the interval to a major 2nd (e.g., A
to B). Now, decrease the interval to the
minor 2nd (e.g., A to Bb). Finally, try a
very minute change in pitch...about a 1/4
tone or less. The fluctuation in pitch
should not be obvious.

Like all the other vocal skills, throat
vibrato is more easily controlled when
there is a balanced foundation of support,
focus and open resonating space. Again, we
recommend using abdominal vibrato for almost all applications.

HELPFUL HINTS

    1. If you find you cannot speed up the
diaphragmatic vibrato and you feel that you
are laboring at it, you are probably pump-
ing the pulses too hard and allowing the
support to relax between pulses. Do not
force or jerk the pulses. This will actually drag down the speed.

    2. Let the tone flow out and forward.
Don't think 'up and down'.

    3. Don't allow any other parts of the
body to pulse along with the vibrato,
(head, jaw, etc.). Use your fingertips to
check that your support is not obviously
pulsing with the vibrato.

    4. If you are having trouble keeping
the vibrato smooth, re-emphasize the steady
support without increasing air pressure.

    5. Ultimately, when the balance is
achieved, it takes merely subtle pulses to
produce the desired effect. The result is a
vibrato that feels natural, free and.....
'On The Breath'.

BACKGROUND ON VIBRATO

Vibrato is used in all or most classical singing but prior to 1700, the 'pure' straight tone was preferred. The straight tone in singing was characteristic of Renaissance music and earlier works such as the Gregorian Chant and is still performed in that manner today. Approaching the nineteenth century, the vocal repertoire of the Romantic period began to reflect more emotional realism ('Verismo'), as in the operas..*Pagliacci*, *Cavalleria Rusticana* and *La Bohème*. Vibrato became popular as a sensual enhancement of the vocal sound and became the throb in the heart beat of Romantic style. It is inconceivable that an aria by Verdi or Puccini would be performed without vibrato.

In opera, the type of vibrato varies from one culture to another. A slightly wider and slower vibrato is more typical of the Italian style of singing, compared to the faster and narrower vibrato of the French and German style.

Opera singers of the German style, especially when interpreting the operas of Richard Wagner and Richard Strauss, often use a straight tone, moving into a quick, narrow vibrato. The effect is a piercing, intense quality, well suited to the heroic roles of 20th Century German Opera. Wagner wrote for the voice as if it were one of the instruments in the total musical fabric. Because of the tremendous size of the orchestra used in some of these works, the vibrato described above, coupled with a sizable voice, became necessary for projection. This use of the vibrato assists the singer in penetrating and soaring above the orchestra.

The faster vibrato evolved into an even more rapid 'vocal cord' vibrato in the contemporary style of the French chanteuse or cabaret singer, such as Edith Piaf. The Flamenco singer of Spain, as well as many of the Mid-Eastern singers (Israeli and Arabic), also use a fast vocal cord or throat vibrato, compared to the slower vibrato of most American singers.

The straight tone, used intermittently with a very slow and somewhat wide vibrato, is typical of the Japanese pop singer. Not too long ago, we were working with two Japanese singers who were sent to New York on a government grant to study voice and theater arts. When they returned to Japan, they were complimented on their authentic 'American sound'. Their vibrato control made the difference.

* **Placement**

* **Resonance**

* **Vocal Colors**

Just like all acoustic instruments; guitar, trumpet, piano, violin, etc., the voice has its own special chambers for resonating the tone. Once the tone is produced by the vibrating vocal cords, it is aimed or "placed" to activate the four basic reson- ance colors (head, nasal, mouth, chest) in a variety of combinations.

Generally speaking, we think of the various resonances as the vocal colors in a spec- trum; a continuous range from dark to bright. There is a natural shift through this spectrum or "resonance track", with the chest resonance (dark color) predom- inating in the lower notes; in the middle range, the mouth/nasal resonance is domin- ant; in the higher range, the head/nasal resonance (bright color) predominates. The objective is to have command of all the colors of the spectrum which allows you, the artist, greater scope of emotional expression.

   HEAD RESONANCE — Used primarily for softer singing ("head tones").

   NASAL RESONANCE — Used at all times ex- cept, perhaps, in the instance of the pure head tone; nasal resonance is bright and 'edgy'; used in combination with mouth resonance to create forward placement; well suited to zany character voices. In an over-all sense, it adds overtones that enrich the vocal sound.

MOUTH RESONANCE — Used for a 'conversational' vocal color; used in combination with nasal resonance, to create forward placement.

CHEST RESONANCE — Emphasized for deeper and richer tone coloring.

<u>Allow the word or emotional content of the phrase to suggest the color and/or volume of the tone.</u>

There are some singers who are recognized by their pronounced nasal quality and others noted for a deep, dark and 'chesty' sound and still others for their breathy or heady sound...and so on. Such individuality depends also on the structure of the singer's vocal instrument, the inherent shape and size of the vocal cords, resonance chambers, etc. This has been scientifically demonstrated electrographically in the form of 'voiceprints' which show that, like fingerprints, no two voices are exactly alike.

These various resonances may be emphasized or blended by altering the shape and size of the chambers through which the sound travels.

Exercises for Placement

NASAL RESONANCES

****
To assist in accomplishing the FORWARD
PLACEMENT, place your finger tips gently
along side your nose and aim the vocal tone
as if to vibrate against your fingers. It
is also helpful to aim the tone out against
the top front teeth.
****

The "aa" vowel sound (as in 'at') is the
most conducive to opening the nasal
resonance and achieving forward placement. The consonants N, M and NG assist
the process since they require nasal
opening.

1. Think the sound "ng" (as in
'angle') and say: "aaaaa, aaaaa, aaaaa".

Notice that thinking "ng" brings the
tongue closer than necessary to the soft
palate, but this allows the nasal
resonance to be felt more easily since
the tone is partly channeled through the
nasal passage.

2. Repeat the above exercise without
bringing the tongue close to the soft
palate. Feel for the same open nasal
resonance.

3. Say: "nyaaa ,nyaaa, nyaaa"

Say: "naa, naa, naa"

A pure nasal tone is very rarely used
except for character voices or "special

effects".

> 4. Repeat #3, singing on a com-
fortable pitch with vibrato.

              nya-a-a-a-a-a-a-a-a
               (～～～～～～～～～)
              na-a-a-a-a-a-a-a-a
               (～～～～～～～～)

> 5. Using "aaaaa" as a model, sing
various words containing the 'aa' vowel,
like "land":

              la-a-a-a-a-a-a-a-and
               (～～～～～～～～～)

"grass":

              gra-a-a-a-a-a-a-a-ass
               (～～～～～～～～～)

> 6. Sing:
>   eh (as in 'end')
         aa...aa...e-e-e-e-e-e-e-e-eh

Continue with other vowel sounds using
the list on page 14.

> 7. Using Ex. #1, p. 112, sing:

    '...now and then and...'
       (2 notes per word)

> 8. Continue with the list of "prac-
tice phrases" (p. 113), without losing
the presence of the nasal placement.

HEAD RESONANCE

Yawn and feel the sensation at the back of
your mouth as the space widens between the
back of your tongue and the roof of your
mouth. (Don't pull your tongue back.) This
assists in relaxing the focusing strength
of the cords for softer tones.

1. With the yawn sensation, listen
for a sound that is light, "heady" and
clearly focused (not breathy). Use a
firm out and down support but very little air pressure. Feel the cords vibrate
gently and say:

"ooooo" (like an owl in the distance)

This helps emphasize and identify the head
resonance. At lower volumes, the "oo" or
"ee" sounds are most conducive to the
"head" resonance.

The tip of the tongue should rest behind
the lower teeth except to move away momentarily to articulate consonants like
"t", "d", "l", "n", "sh", etc..

2. Sing on a comfortable pitch and
use the delayed vibrato:

oo (as in 'moon'):

Mooooo-oo-oo-oo-oo-oon
(————————~~~~~~~~~~)

ah (as in 'honor'):

aaaaaa-a-a-a-a-ah
(————————~~~~~~~)

After you establish these head tones try
other vowel sounds, then words. When a word
starts with a vowel, begin the tone with a
"silent H" to avoid a cough-like popping of
the vocal cords, or 'glottal attack'.

      3. Match the 'heady' quality of the
"ee" and "oo" in the vowel of the word
that follows.

      'ah' vowel sound (in 'gone')
          ee...ee...ga-a-a-a-a-a-a-a-ahn
          oo...oo...ga-a-a-a-a-a-a-a-ahn
                (∿∿∿∿∿∿∿∿)

          ee...ee...hello-o-o-o-o-o-o-o-oh
          oo...oo...hello-o-o-o-o-o-o-o-oh

      4. Using exercise #1 (page 112, soft
only), sing:

      '...you and me and...'
       (2 notes per word)

      5. Continue, using the 'practice
phrases' (p. 113).

MOUTH RESONANCE

      1. With a natural, hearty, speech-
like quality, say "Hi!".

Feel the open vowel sound vibrating against
the upper front teeth. An open mouth, as if
you are about to bite an apple, slightly
baring the upper teeth, facilitates a clear
vowel and forward placement. This mouth
position prevents "covering" or trapping
the sound.

      2. Say: "Hey!" (against the teeth)

3. Sing on a single sustained tone with 9 pulses of vibrato:

Hey: He-e-e-e-e-e-e-e-ehee
        (∿∿∿∿∿∿∿∿∿)

Why: Wha-a-a-a-a-a-a-a-ahee
        (∿∿∿∿∿∿∿∿∿)

4. Move on to other vowel sounds ...words such as "go", "seem", "storm" etc..

5. Using exercise #1 (a-d), page 112, sing:

'...on and on and...'
  (one note per word)

6. Continue, using the 'practice phrases' (p. 113).

Speak these sounds at first and then go on to sustain a tone on a pitch. When emphasizing the mouth resonance, you should feel the presence of the other resonances, particularly nasal and chest.

CHEST RESONANCE

The chest resonance, added to the other vocal colors, accomplishes maximum "depth" and richness of tone. Be aware of the tendency to relax focusing strength when increasing the space in the throat for chest color. Keep that "buzz" of mask resonance in the sound and don't push the air pressure beyond good balance.

1. 'Think' the sound "uh" as in "under" and call out "Whoa!"...like calling a horse to stop.

Vibrations can be felt in the chest area

while the tone projects out through and
mixes with the mask resonance. You will
feel the back of your tongue lower as you
say the 'uh' sound but don't let it pull
back into the throat. Be careful to maintain focus and forward placement as you
widen the throat space. In some cases, it
takes time to learn to focus well for the
very dark tones. The forward placement
(mouth/nasal) wonderfully balances the
chest sound, making it even richer by
adding the higher overtones.

    2. Using exercise #1 (a-d) on page
112, sing "Whoa!".

    3. On a comfortable pitch in the
lower range, sing with 9 pulses of
vibrato (loud then soft):

    'whoa!'

      wo-o-o-o-o-o-o-o-oh
    (~~~~~~~~~~~~)

    'my'

      ma-a-a-a-a-a-a-ahee
    (~~~~~~~~~~~~)

    4. Using exercise #1(a-d), page 112,
sing:

    '...so and so and...'

It is quite natural and appropriate for all
the resonances to be active and a skillful
artist can emphasize or blend the vocal
colors to suit the emotional expression.

HELPFUL HINTS:

1. BE CAREFUL: When emphasizing the chest resonance on higher notes (especially louder), keep the air pressure within the limits of good balance. Don't push.

2. Stay on top of the pitch as there is a tendency to sing under the pitch when emphasizing chest color in the higher range.

3. When experimenting with volume control in the various resonances, keep the vocal color constant as you vary volume.

4. For greatest volume, emphasize chest resonance along with all the other resonances. DON'T PUSH! The chest color is independent of volume.

5. When making a smooth transition into the upper register, it is necessary to modify volume (see pp. 48 - 56).

The "BREAK"

Registers

Most male and female voices experience two distinct ranges or registers; <u>lower regis-ter</u> (also called chest voice, lower voice, alto, 'belt') and <u>upper register</u> (head voice, upper voice, 'legit' voice, soprano, falsetto). Falsetto is a term more commonly associated with the upper register of the male voice which resembles the female so-prano quality.

It is common to experience an abrupt change in the vocal sound when moving from one register to the other. This change or "break" takes place in the area where the registers overlap. Notes within the overlap area are usually sung either in the higher part of the chest register or in the lower part of the head register. However, in this area of transition, sometimes called the "passaggio", a blending or 'mixing' of the registers is possible and can be learned.

<u>To make a smooth transition</u> into the upper register, do not reach a volume level that requires air pressure great enough to push the vocal cords open. Because the vocal cords require less focusing strength for the lower notes of the head register, excessive pressure pushes them open, unfo-cusing the voice, causing sudden breath-iness. This effect (or defect) is more apparent the louder you sing while making

the upward transition. In other words, if you are singing too loud in the upper chest while moving into the head register, you will be unable to match the vocal qualities. For most voices, the chest voice can sing louder than the head voice on notes within the overlap area, making the register break an almost universal experience.

When making the <u>downward transition</u> from the head voice, one tendency is to carry the upper register too low, resulting in a sense of weakness, breathiness or cracking in the vocal sound. This usually prompts the unskilled singer to over-compensate by suddenly increasing air pressure and focusing strength, causing an abrupt change into lower register.

You will also experience a "break" if you are not supporting well enough as you move down from head voice into the upper chest. The throat will suddenly tighten, interfering with forward placement and/or pitch. It could even 'grab' tightly enough to choke off the sound completely.

Now, we will explore the techniques by which you can.............

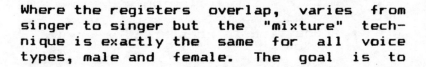

Fix It Yourself

Where the registers overlap, varies from singer to singer but the "mixture" technique is exactly the same for all voice types, male and female. The goal is to match the qualities of one register to the other, which may involve some practice to get the right 'feel'.

A sudden vocal change or 'break' will not occur <u>anywhere</u> in the vocal range if you maintain:

1. Steady support

2. Clear focus

3. Pure vowel

4. Forward placement

'Pop' Sound Upper Mixture

For a strong Pop or Rock sound when moving upward through the passaggio, maintain the mouth/nasal emphasis and focusing strength. You can create the impression that your chest voice comfortably reaches the high notes. Don't go into pure head resonance. To 'mellow' the sound, add some chest color without adding volume.

Gospel singers, like Aretha Franklin, often use this technique to carry the chest sound up into the soprano or falsetto range for emotional intensity.

NOTE: The following exercises are also helpful in strengthening the upper register of the classical female voice (i.e., 'legit' soprano, mezzo, contralto).

NOTE: For the following exercises, do not exceed medium volume until your register transition is consistently smooth.

EXERCISES:

1. On the sound "ny<u>aa</u>" as in "hat", slide your voice on a siren-like tone, beginning in the lower part of the voice and proceeding slowly and smoothly to the highest part of the range and back.

Without ever losing forward placement or purity of vowel, feel a gradual shift along the resonance track: chest-mouth-nasal-head-nasal-mouth-chest.

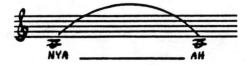

NYA _____ AH

The objective here is to eliminate any abrupt changes in volume, focus, placement, vowel clarity, support or vocal color. Don't give in to the tendency to relax support on the downward slide. Use your finger tips to check.

2. Beginning on a note in your upper middle range, sing this downward arpeggio, as single notes (staccato) and then connected (legato) on "aa". Aim for a pure 'aa' (as in 'at').

3. Repeat exercise #2 a half step higher each time. Gradually increase the

head/nasal emphasis as you move your
voice higher.

If you're experiencing a glottal attack,
approach the beginning of the vowel with a
'silent H' (see p. 23).

   4. Sustain each note in the following exercise with 6 pulses of vibrato
using the word sounds below:

   aa(as in 'at')
      nyaaaaaaaaaaaaaaaaaaaaaaaaa

   ehee(as in 'nay')
      neeeeeeeeeeeeeeeeeeeeeeeehee

   5. Repeat, using the phrases on page
113.

   6. Try different volume levels.

   7. Continue to develop your mixture
with these more advanced exercises:

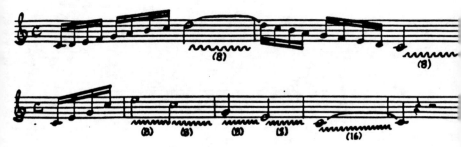

Keep practicing these exercises until you have mastered the blend from lower register, through mixture, into upper register and back down with smoothness. Match the tone quality and maintain the pure vowel throughout. You should not feel any abrupt changes anywhere in your range.

At first the mixture may seem a little unstable but with practice, you will be able to improve your co-ordination, controlling a continuous balance of SUPPORT, FOCUS, PURE VOWEL and FORWARD PLACEMENT. This balance in motion will feel more and more natural and the break will disappear.

Classical Sound
Lower Mixture

Here, we are interested in using the mix as a downward extention of the classical or 'legit' soprano sound (including mezzo and contralto). In general, the movement from the soprano or 'legit' sound into the lower mixture takes place approximately between A above middle C and the D below that.

EXERCISES:

       1. On the vowel 'ah'(as in 'hot'), sing:

       2. Repeat, beginning a half step lower each time.

As you begin the descending scale, grad- ually increase the chest resonance (use the 'yawn'), maintaining a balance between air pressure and focused vocal cords. Be care- ful not to lose forward placement when em- phasizing chest color. With each successive note, match the sound and feeling of the previous tone. Keep support steady. Keep the vowel clearly pronounced which helps stabilize the voice through the passaggio.

       3. Following the above instructions, sing:

       4. Using exercise #5, on page 112, first, sing vowels and then 'practice phrases', page 113.

       5. Continue developing your mixture using the above exercises, #1 - 4.

HELPFUL HINTS:

1. Increase the open jaw space for the higher notes but don't stretch to the limit. Opening too wide will tend to cause tension in the jaw and tighten the throat, cutting off forward placement. Open comfortably wide (about an inch).

2. Feel a smile in your sound; not so much an outer facial expression but an "inner smile". This "inner smile" activates the "mask" resonances.

3. Use a mirror, now and then, to be sure your tongue is relaxed down and forward. Pulling your tongue back destroys the forward placement and vowel purity.

4. Don't think in terms of reaching for a note; up or down. Think smooth, continuous outward flow of sound.

5. There is a tendency to over emphasize or accent the top note of a scale or phrase. Practice a smooth, even vocal line. Reserve accents for emotional impact.

6. Keep the support steady and firm on the descending scale or melody.

7. If there is an abrupt change into the chest voice, this could be due to a sudden tightening or "grabbing" of the throat muscles, often the result of trying to move into the chest voice too high in the range.

8. If there is an abrupt change into the head voice, you may be singing too loud and/or bringing chest voice too high as you attempt the transition.

Staccato

The staccato is a short detached note, written with a dot above it to indicate a reduction of its written duration by half or more.

The same abdominal pulses that you use for diaphragmatic vibrato are used for staccato. But unlike the vibrato which is a continuous tone, the staccato has distinct breaks between successive tones.

    1. On the vowel 'ah' (as in 'on') sing:

    2. Repeat, beginning a half step higher each time.

3. Sing:

HELPFUL HINTS:

1. Keep support steady. Don't relax between staccato tones. Use your finger-tips to check.

2. Imagine the pulse as centered in the solar plexus area or mid-section.

3. Keep the vowel pure.

4. Avoid glottal attack. Don't close the throat space between tone pulses.

5. Although the individual pitches and rhythms must be accurate, the flow of the whole phrase is the primary con-sideration.

The Trill

The trill is a rapid, even fluctuation of pitch, either a Major 2nd (whole step in-terval) or a minor 2nd (half step):

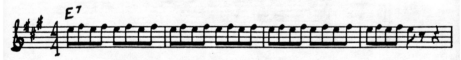

whole step trill

half step trill

In the score, it is the lower note of the trill that is written with the trill symbol above it:

An average pulse rate for the trill is similar to that of the vibrato; about 5 to 9 per second (2 notes per pulse). To trill, use the same action as in the throat vibrato but equally emphasize both upper and lower pitches. It is helpful to 'think' the upper pitch in order to counteract the tendency to emphasize the lower pitch.

Often the trill begins slowly and speeds up.

    1. On 'ah', sing:

    2. Now sing the trill beginning with the sixteenth notes.

✻ Do It With ✻
✻ Style ✻

The vocal technique described in the previous section will keep your voice healthy
and give you the control to bring out the
creative artist within you. In this section, we will study:

1) VOCAL STYLES
2) PERSONAL STYLE and PERFORMANCE

<u>Vocal colors</u>, <u>volume dynamics</u>, <u>vibrato</u>
<u>Phrasing</u>, <u>improvisation</u> and <u>pronunciation</u>
are the building blocks of vocal style. In
each style — Rhythm & Blues, Country, Rock,
Broadway, Jazz and Classical — there are
recognizable differences in the way singers
use these elements. Let's explore.

BLUES

A great proportion of "Pop" songs of the
20th Century — Country, Pop, Rock, Gospel,
Rhythm & Blues and Jazz — are influenced by
the Blues. Since much of the melodic expression and improvisation in this music
contain elements of the Blues scale, it is
extremely valuable for singers to be familiar with it.

Train yourself to sing the Blues scale
beginning on any starting note, both ascending and descending.

Beginning on any note, the intervals of the Blues scale are: minor 3rd (1-1/2 steps), Major 2nd (whole step), minor 2nd (1/2 step), minor 2nd (1/2 step), minor 3rd (1-1/2 steps), Major 2nd (whole step).

Using the minor scale as a base, the notes of a Blues scale are as follows:

One good way to think of it is: 1-3-4 in A minor and 1-3-4 in E minor with a half step in between (D#): [A-C-D-D#-E-G-A].

For a Blues influence on the Major scale, add the flatted 3rd, 5th and 7th. The singer often "bends" the notes, moving between the natural and flatted. The flat-ted 3rd, 5th and 7th (which are not always printed) are "Blue" notes.

By listening and singing with Blues artists you will get the feel of it...Ray Charles, Billie Holliday, Mose Allison, etc..

   1. Choose a pitch. Using the Blues scale, sing: ('doot - doot' - etc.)

   1-3-4-4#-5-7-8(✓)8-7-5-4#-4-3-1.

   Sing these Blues melodies:

   1-8-7-4#-4-3-1

   1-3-1-4#-4-3-1

   1-4#-5-7-5-7-8

8-4#-5-7-5-4-4#-4-3-1

2. Choose another starting pitch and repeat exercise #1 (above).

3. Sing:

Your intonation (ability to sing pitches accurately in tune) must be perfected. If one note is off, it tends to throw the next note off and so on. Be especially careful of the accuracy of the half steps in the descending line.

Use the Blues scale to exercise your voice in all parts of the range to develop your ear and vocal co-ordination.

Here's a phrase in the Rhythm & Blues style as it appears in the sheet music:

A singer familiar with the Blues scale can transform that simple phrase into this soulful expression:

Here's a Country phrase in its simple form, as written:

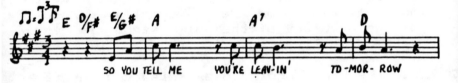

Here it is again with some Blue notes added:

Here's a phrase from a Rock ballad in its simple form, as written:

COMES A TIME   IN YOUR LIFE WHEN YOU KNOW__ITS AL-RIGHT

Here's that phrase again with added notes
and hidden notes from the Blues scale.
(hidden/grace/passing note: added note of
short duration, subtle to the ear)

♪ = HIDDEN NOTE (GRACE NOTE)

COMES A TIME   IN YOUR LIFE WHEN YOU

KNOW IT'S   AL __ RIGHT

As you play with the Blues scale, you will
love creating your own melodies. Experiment
with improvising and have fun!

Play the above measures (on piano, guitar,
etc.) repeatedly (or use the accompaniments
on Tape III, side A; Tape IV, side B -- see
p. 125) and sing your own improvised melodies in the Blues style. Work slowly at
first and give your full range a work-out.
Here's your big chance to "wail"...use that
falsetto!

Blue notes are not the only notes added to melodies for greater emotional expression. Here's a phrase in Country style in its simple form, as written:

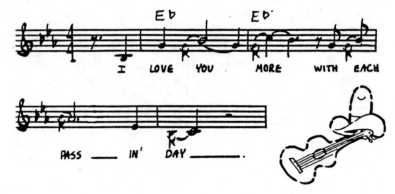

Here it is again, embellished with added notes:

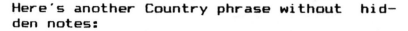

Here's another Country phrase without hidden notes:

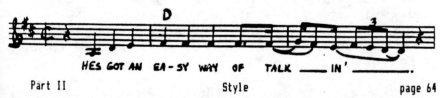

Here it is with added melody notes. Notice how this brings out the Country flavor. The group of added notes is often called a "lick".

Sing these phrases slowly at first, gradually speeding up to an appropriate tempo.
Keep it 'clean'...on pitch.

Here's a phrase in the R&B or Soul style,
as written:

Now, here it is with some *style*. Notice the
lick on the word "cry" which increases the
emotional impact of the word.

In this set of examples, notice how you can
enrich the character and emotional content
with a lick on the word "man".

Here's a set of phrases in Rock style, simple and embellished:

Here's another set of Rock style phrases:

ROCK
PENTATONIC SCALE

Like the Blues scale, the Pentatonic scale
is a strong influence on the sound of Rock
music. But Rock is a very broad category.
We have seen Hard Rock, Soft Rock, Jazz
Rock, Rock-A-Billy, Classical Rock, Heavy
Metal, Rock'N'Roll, Southern Rock, Folk
Rock and more.

As the name, "Pentatonic" suggests, this is
a 5 note scale. If you play only the black
notes on the piano, you will be playing the
notes of a Pentatonic scale. (whole step,
1-1/2, whole, whole, 1-1/2)

Here's a Rock phrase
using the Pentatonic scale.

Notice the Blue note on the word, "baby" in
the second example. Feel free to use elements of both Blues and Pentatonic scales
to add dimension to your Rock style. (see
p. 84)

Phrasing and Improvising

Phrasing refers to the way in which a singer groups and emphasizes the lyrics of a
song. Improvising in a song is inventing or
creating melodies that vary from the original melody line. These improvisations may
be similar to the original or they could be
quite different; in any case, they must be
harmonically compatible with the chord progression (chord changes).

Though there is a variety of other scales,
your familiarity with the Major, minor,

Blues and Pentatonic gives you everything you need to improvise. Make your words, phrases, 'intros', 'breaks' (instrumental interludes), repeated sections, endings and 'repeat and fade' endings all come alive with a professional touch.

The following examples illustrate how you can re-phrase and improvise to enhance and heighten emotional impact:

Sing: (Country style)

Sing: (Rhythm & Blues style)

INVENTIVE PHRASING

When repeating a phrase in a song, you can
add excitement by improvising increasingly
elaborate melodies. Here is the above melody as it might be sung the second or third
time.

The following are progressively energetic
variations on a simple melody.

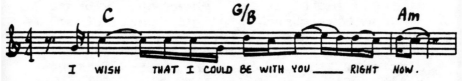

 JAZZ

Free-style, spontaneous phrasing is one of the trademarks of Jazz singers. They embellish the lyrics with melodic and rhythmic invention and even "scat" improvised melodies, replacing the words with word/sounds. Such artists include Ella Fitzgerald, Al Jarreau and Louis Armstrong to name a few.

Singers interested in specializing in Jazz and general improvisational style should listen to and sing along with the greats, including instrumentalists like Oscar Peterson, John Coltrane, Pete Fountain and others. Their use of phrasing, vibrato, resonance (timbre), straight tone, attacks and releases greatly influence Jazz singers, who imitate the sounds of the trumpet, clarinet, flute, saxaphone, etc.. Flexibility and a variety of vocal colors are features of the Jazz sound/style, encompassing a wide range of effects.

To develop more sophisticated improvisational skills, you also need to familiarize yourself with the many scales, in addition to those found in this book, that are common to the Jazz idiom. There are excellent music theory books available that treat the subject of Jazz Improvisation.

MUSICAL THEATER

Musical Theater repertoire does not generally allow flexibility in phrasing or improvisation. The stage director, composer
and musical director ordinarily have the
final word on tempo, dynamics and general
interpretation. Improvisational choices may
be made during rehearsal, but become estab-
lished and set by opening night. This usually sets a precedent for future perfor-
mances. You might actually disappoint your
audience if you don't adhere to the original interpretation of the song. Naturally,
you will have more freedom if <u>you</u> are the
originator of the role.

OPERA

Phrasing is even more strict in Opera,
where the composer has set down the notes,
rhythms, tempos and dynamics, all of which
must be sung precisely by the performer
under the guidance of the conductor. Notes
and words are not usually changed to suit
the singer. However, some artists have de-
viated from the written notes and by the
power of their virtuosity and popularity,
have creatively embellished the text, es-
tablishing new interpretations which subse-
quently have become traditional.

COLORATURA, the use of rapid melodic passa-
ges for embellishment, including scales,
arpeggios, trills and staccati, is part of
an operatic style most evident in the works
of composers such as Rossini, Donizetti and
Bellini. These melodic variations, written
or improvised, are often sung in a repeated
section or ending of an aria ('cadenza')
for emphasis, playfulness or to show off
the singer's virtuosity.

The FERMATA (⌢•) indicates that the note
below it is to be sustained longer than
written. How long?...at the discretion of
the singer or conductor. Sometimes this
liberty is taken without the fermata. For
example, in his first Act aria of <u>La
Boheme</u>, Rodolfo holds his high C as long as
he thinks he can...which is usually about 8
times longer than written. Audiences know
when that high C is coming and very anx-
iously await the moment...evaluating and
comparing it to all the high Cs they've ever heard.

The CADENCE or CADENZA is an elaborate melodic embellishment either written by the
composer or created by the singer. It occurs at the end of a section or at the con-
clusion of an aria to add excitement and to
show off the singer's artistry. The cadenza
is usually sung over the chord preceeding
the final chord. The conductor often gives
the singer great freedom to interpret the
cadenza, sometimes even taking the cue from
the singer for the downbeat of the resolv-
ing chord. The cadenza may take the form of
scales, arpeggios and/or trills; sung detached (staccato) and/or smoothly (legato).
Although the cadenza is set and well re-
hearsed, it should seem to be a free flowing flourish of spontaneous vocal expression.

coloratura embellishment

PHRASING GUIDELINES:

In all areas of Pop music, singers have great freedom to vary from the written notes, rhythms and phrasing. The notes on the page may be just a framework on which to build your interpretation. You're given the notes and words but very little, if anything, about phrasing, licks, dynamics or vocal colors. These elements are left up to you, the artist.

    1. The most effective method for find- ing expressive phrasing is to <u>speak the words</u> of each phrase, not just mechanically reciting the lyric but letting your emo- tions flow. Notice your rhythms, inflec- tions and accents. Transfer these choices to your singing and you will see how easy and natural it feels and sounds.

    2. If a word occurs on a downbeat, you can 'anticipate' by singing the word <u>before</u> the downbeat, or 'back-phrase', lagging be- hind the beat.

    3. Always be aware of the chord changes accompanying the melody of the phrase since too much play or flexibility in the phrasing may cause you to sound as though you are not 'in sync' with your accom- paniment or off pitch.

    4. You are not obligated to sustain a word that is written to be held. You could choose another word to sustain if it makes more sense to you.

    5. You may sing a phrase in <u>less</u> time than indicated on the sheet music and make up for it by <u>stretching</u> out the following phrase or vice-versa.

Pronunciation

Pronunciation should fit the style. For the most part, in "popular" songs people are speaking to people about familiar feelings and experiences. Singers in all areas of "Pop" music generally use natural conversational and regional pronunciation. For example, to sing Country music with authenticity, a singer would have to have or learn that "down home" pronunciation.

Classical and Musical Theater singers generally use a more formal, standard stage diction, unless the characterization calls for a dialect.

Individuality

Turn on the radio and you hear the sound of Johnny Cash or Streisand or Rod Stewart or Ella. You recognize the voice almost immediately by its unique sound or style.

Some important factors that determine vocal individuality are: physical structure of the vocal apparatus (genetic), environmental input, positive or negative feedback, singing experience and training.

No two voices, even in the case of identical twins, are exactly alike. From birth, voices, like fingerprints, are measurably different from one another and also like fingerprints, may be graphically represented in the form of 'voiceprints', demonstrating their uniqueness.

From birth, our unique instruments are vehicles for expression, influenced by environmental input. The music we hear and the musical attitudes of those around us affect our tastes, our way of listening and even our self-confidence. Young children, experimenting with singing, who receive positive re-enforcement and encouragement for their little shows of ability, may well become what we call, "a natural", free and uninhibited. On the other hand, those receiving negative feedback, may develop a block about singing, manifested as a 'pitch problem' ('tin ear'), poor sense of rhythm, unmusical voice quality and a general avoidance of singing due to a lack of confidence.

We have worked with thousands of voices, from Rock'N'Roll to Opera, from beginners to seasoned professionals, from children of 3 to seniors of 74, and we have found that song styling is a wonderful musical adventure for those inspired enough to keep at it. It tends to be easier and seems more natural the earlier you begin. How early? ....As early as learning to speak. And like learning to speak, we learn to sing by listening and imitating. It is often without awareness that we 'study' and absorb the styles of our favorite singers.....the way they use:

> Phrasing
> Licks
> Improvisation
> Pronunciation
> Vibrato
> Vocal Colors
> Volume Dynamics

Developing
Personal Style

The process of listening and imitating is the most effective and possibly the only way of learning any style. Your own personal style will evolve naturally as you continue to sing with a variety of vocal artists. Here are some guide lines:

1. Choose a recorded rendition of a song by an artist you admire. Make sure that the recording is in a comfortable key for your own voice. You may have to search to find the right song.

2. Sing along with the song, copying every nuance; resonances, vibrato, dynamics, licks, etc..

3. After you have mastered the song to the best of your ability, go on to another song. Don't use the same artist for more than three or four songs in succession.

4. Choose other artists, repeating this approach.

Believe it or not, your own style will naturally evolve. You will automatically pick up and retain those qualities which suit your voice and personality and leave behind those characteristics that do not.

This is also an excellent technique for learning a new style. For example, if your main focus has been on Broadway music, and you would like to learn a Pop style, listening to and singing along with Pop singers is the best approach. If you are a Pop singer with a desire to sing Jazz, listen to and sing along with Jazz artists. Working this way, the differences among styles will become obvious and you will be able to apply the techniques you've learned in new ways.

Good vocal technique alone will not automatically make you a successful performer. A willingness to communicate your feelings, coupled with vocal control, is the necessary combination that can make you a powerful and charismatic artist. Your technique should be an invisible part of the musical fabric, interwoven with emotions that penetrate the heart and soul of your audience. TECHNIQUE SERVES ART.

Your audience will be emotionally moved, if you are emotionally moved. Technique, without committment produces a mechanical and untruthful performance. A stirring performance requires a personal, emotional commitment to the story in the song. Become that person in the song just as a good actor becomes the character he or she plays.

DO IT WITH STYLE!

✻ Sight—Singing ✻
✻ Ear—Training ✻

Scales

THE MAJOR SCALE

Every Major scale has a KEY SIGNATURE de-
signating its sharps or flats. It appears
immediately following the G clef (treble
clef) at the beginning of the piece. These
sharps or flats serve to maintain the relationship of whole and half steps in the
scale. The half steps fall between the 3rd
and 4th and the 7th and 8th degrees of the
scale. All the other intervals are whole
steps. (see keyboard chart, pg. 80) This
relationship gives the scale the Major
sound.

For example, if the key is G Major, the F#
in the key signature tells you that every
"F" throughout the entire piece is sharped
unless otherwise indicated. This avoids
having to place a sharp before each and
every F in the piece.

Memorize the number of sharps and flats in
each key and the order in which they follow
one another. The order is easy to remember
using a system called "circle of 5ths" or
"circle of 4ths".

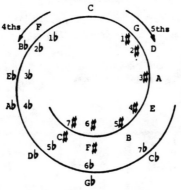

<u>Order of Flats</u>, (circle of 4ths):

Bb, Eb, Ab, Db, Gb, Cb, Fb

<u>B</u>ig <u>E</u>aters <u>A</u>lways <u>D</u>ig <u>G</u>ood <u>C</u>hinese <u>F</u>ood.

<u>Order of Sharps</u>, (circle of 5ths):

F#, C#, G#, D#, A#, E#, B#

<u>F</u>at <u>C</u>ats <u>G</u>o <u>D</u>ancing <u>A</u>t <u>E</u>rnie's <u>B</u>ar.

A <u>Major</u> scale consists of 8 notes, 5 whole
steps and 2 half steps. (pp. 115-118)

A <u>minor</u> scale, in its natural   form, also
consists of 8 notes, 5 whole steps and 2
half steps. (p. 81)

It is necessary that a singer be able to
differentiate between the sound of the
<u>whole</u> step and the <u>half</u> step.

Sing:

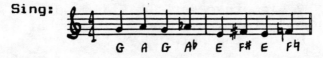

<u>Half</u> step: Note to note, without skipping a note. (C-Db; A-G#; F-E; Bb-A)

<u>Whole</u> step: Note to note, skipping a note (C-D; D-E; F#-G#; Ab-Bb).

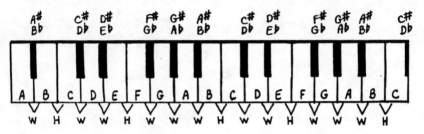

Note: W = whole step
H = half step

To raise a note one half step, add a sharp sign (#) before the note on the staff. To raise a note two half steps, add a double sharp sign (X) before the note.

To lower a note one half step, place a flat sign (♭) before the note. When lowering a note two half steps, place a double flat (♭♭) before the note.

The double sharps and flats are more common to Classical and Jazz notation and rarely appear in Pop music.

Examples:

The sharped or flatted note, specified by the key signature may be altered to its "natural" state, by placing a natural sign (♮) before the note.

These symbols are called "accidentals". The accidental alters the pitch for the duration of the measure in which it appears unless a new accidental is indicated.

Example:

THE MINOR SCALE

Every Major scale has a "relative minor" scale which, in its natural form, has the same sharps or flats as its "relative Major". The relative minor scale may be found by descending one and one half steps from the first degree of the Major scale and is three letter names away. Examples: C Major-A minor; G Major-E minor, Db Major-Bb minor; Gb Major-Eb minor. In the minor scale, unlike the Major, the half steps fall between the 2nd and 3rd and between the 5th and 6th degrees of the scale. This is the "natural minor" scale:

'A' natural minor scale

There are two other forms of minor scales.

HARMONIC MINOR SCALE

Simply raise the 7th of the natural minor scale one half step.

'A' harmonic minor scale

MELODIC MINOR SCALE

Raise the 6th and 7th of the natural minor scale one-half step when ascending the scale and use the natural minor scale when descending.

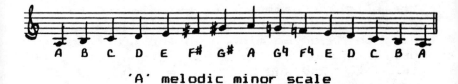

'A' melodic minor scale

It is valuable to know the key signatures (sharps or flats) of every Major and minor scale. The most commonly used keys do not exceed four sharps or flats, especially in Pop music. The Classical or Jazz singer is more likely to encounter a wider variety of keys.

    In the following exercise, use numbers 1 through 8, for the notes of the scale.

Sing the words, "one" – "two" – etc.:

```
1 2 3 4 5 6 7 8 - 8 7 6 5 4 3 2 1
1 2 3 4 5 6 7 - 7 6 5 4 3 2 1
1 2 3 4 5 6 - 6 5 4 3 2 1
1 2 3 4 5 - 5 4 3 2 1
1 2 3 4 - 4 3 2 1
1 2 3 - 3 2 1
1 2 - 2 1
8 7 - 7 8
8 7 6 - 6 7 8
8 7 6 5 - 5 6 7 8
8 7 6 5 4 - 4 5 6 7 8
8 7 6 5 4 3 - 3 4 5 6 7 8
8 7 6 5 4 3 2 - 2 3 4 5 6 7 8
8 7 6 5 4 3 2 1 - 1 2 3 4 5 6 7 8
```

Practice these exercises, first in the
Major, and then in all forms of the minor scales. Also practice the octave:
1 – 8; 8 – 1.

The octave 'jump' is a frequently occur-
ing interval and you should become thor-
oughly familiar with its feeling and
sound. Learn to recognize scale lines by
sound as well as sight. Practice singing
and reading the various scales from the
scale charts (pp. 115–118).

Note: Each degree of the Major and minor
scales has a technical name:
(also see "Intervals", pp.87–95)

1st degree – tonic, or root.

2nd degree – super-tonic (above the tonic).

3rd degree – mediant (mid-way between tonic
and dominant).

4th degree — <u>sub-dominant</u> (<u>under</u> the dominant).

5th degree — <u>dominant</u>.

6th degree — <u>sub-mediant</u> (three notes <u>below</u> the tonic)

7th degree — <u>leading tone</u> — has the quality of leading to the tonic in the Major scale and the Harmonic form of the minor scale. Test this out by singing or playing the Major scale, stopping on the 7th degree. Your musical ear will want to hear the final half step resolution to the root.

THE BLUES SCALE — (see pp 59-66)

THE PENTATONIC SCALE

The Pentatonic scale is a strong influence in Pop music, particularly Rock. The Pentatonic scale consists of five notes. If you play only the black keys on the keyboard, you will hear the sound of a Pentatonic scale (e.g., in the key of C: C-D-F-G-A).

　　　　1. Improvise melodies using only the notes of the Pentatonic scale:

C   D   F   G   A   G♭   A♭   B♭   D♭   E♭

2. Sing this melody:

THE CHROMATIC SCALE

A Chromatic scale is a 12 tone scale, built entirely of half steps, spanning one octave. The notes are sharped when ascending and flatted when descending.

1. Using this Chromatic scale chart, sing the notes ascending and descending.

Because the intervals are all half steps, there is no reference point to establish a sense of the 'tonal center' ("tonic"), making it easy to get lost. So, be precise in your 'intonation' (accuracy of pitch).

2. Sing up and down three consecutive half steps...then four...then five ...etc.. Use a keyboard or other instrument, if possible, to check your intonation.

3. Sing:

It is important to train your ear and singing co-ordination in all the modes (scales)
that we have highlighted here. There are
other modes but these are basic and your
familiarity with them will give you a good
musical foundation.

✳ Intervals ✳

(For the following intervals, refer to the keyboard chart on page 80.)

THE OCTAVE

The octave is an interval of 8 notes; the first and last notes of a Major or a minor scale (C-C, D-D, Ab-Ab, etc.). It is called a 'perfect' interval.

Sing:

THE MAJOR 2nd

A Major 2nd is a <u>whole</u> step interval, note to note, skipping one note in between. Consecutive letter names are used to spell it. For example, the 1st and 2nd degrees of the Major scale are a Major 2nd apart. (C-D, Bb-C, E-F#, B-C#, etc.) Printed on the staff, this interval occurs from line to space or space to line.

THE MINOR 2nd

The minor 2nd is a <u>half</u> step interval; Note
to note, without skipping a note. It must
be spelled using consecutive letter names.
(C-Db, E-F, Bb-Cb, Gb-F) On the staff, this
interval occurs from line to space or space
to line.

Sing:

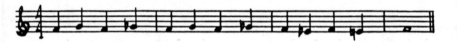

THE MAJOR 3rd

The interval of a Major 3rd may be found by
ascending or descending two whole steps
from any given note. It may be thought of
as the 1st and 3rd degrees of the Major
scale. (C-E, E-G#, G-B, Cb-Eb, etc.) Notice
that the letter names in each example are
three letter names apart. Therefore, this
interval is called a 3rd. It may occur only
from line to line or from space to space on
the staff.

Sing:

THE MINOR 3rd

A minor 3rd may be found by ascending or descending one and one half steps from any given note. It may be thought of as the 1st and 3rd degrees of the minor scale...(A-C, C-Eb, F-Ab, D-F, etc.) This interval may occur only from line to line or from space to space on the staff.

Sing:

    1. Hear and feel the difference between the Major and the minor 3rd:

You can sharpen your ability to harmonize with other singers by becoming familiar with the sound and feel of the Major 3rd and minor 3rd intervals.

2. Play any note on the keyboard and sing a Major 3rd above it; then sing the minor 3rd. Also sing the same intervals downward. Check yourself by playing the note you think you're singing...

        Play C...Sing E...Play E (Major 3rd)
        Play E...Sing G...Play G (minor 3rd)
        Play A...Sing F...Play F (Major 3rd)
        Play F...Sing D...Play D (minor 3rd)
        etc....

    3. Sing this melody:

PERFECT 4th AND PERFECT 5th

The interval of the <u>perfect 4th</u> is the distance between the root and 4th degree of
both the Major and minor scales. The interval of the <u>perfect 5th</u> is the distance between the root and the 5th degree of both
the Major and minor scales.

Sing:

You may <u>widen</u> or "augment" an interval by <u>raising</u> the upper note by one half step or <u>lowering</u> the lower note by one half step. The spelling of the augmented interval must retain its original letter names.

Example: C to F, a perfect 4th, becomes C to F# or Cb to F. These are <u>augmented</u> 4ths. C to G, a perfect 5th, becomes C to G# or Cb to G. These are <u>augmented</u> 5ths:

Sing:

You may also <u>narrow</u> or "diminish" the interval of a perfect 4th or 5th by <u>lowering</u> the upper note one half step or <u>raising</u> the lower note one half step.

Example: C to F, a perfect 4th, becomes C
to Fb or C# to F. These are <u>diminished</u>
4ths. C to G, a perfect 5th becomes C to Gb
or C# to G. These are <u>diminished</u> 5ths.

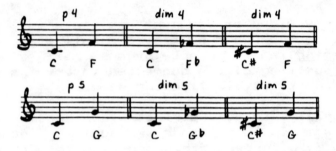

The augmented 4th or diminished 5th interval spans <u>three</u> whole steps and is called a
TRITONE. (C to F#; C to Gb) The tritone is
common in Blues since it is part of the
Blues scale. (<u>1</u>-3-4-<u>4#</u>-5-7-8) The first two
notes of the song, "Maria" from <u>West Side
Story</u>, is also a tritone.

Sing:

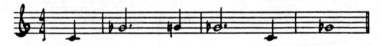

The diminished 4th sounds like a Major 3rd.
(C to Fb sounds like C to E) The Fb and E
are ENHARMONIC, the same pitch spelled two
different ways. The augmented 5th sounds
like a minor 6th. (C to G# sounds like C to
Ab)

MAJOR AND MINOR 6ths

The Major 6th is the interval from the   1st
to the 6th degree of the Major scale.

The minor 6th is the interval from the   1st
to the 6th degree of the minor scale.

    Sing:

MAJOR AND MINOR 7ths

The Major 7th is the interval from the   1st
to the 7th degree of the Major scale.

The minor 7th is the interval from the 1st
to the 7th degree of the minor scale.

Sing:

1. Sing up the Major scale:

1-2-3-4-5-6-7-8
1-8-1-8-1

1-2-3-4-5-6-7
1-7-1-7-1

1-2-3-4-5-6
1-6-1-6-1

1-2-3-4-5
1-5-1-5-1

1-2-3-4
1-4-1-4-1

1-2-3
1-3-1-3-1

1-2-1-2-1

2. Repeat using the minor scale.

As we mentioned earlier, your familiarity
with Major and minor 3rds gives you a good
foundation in vocal harmony. As you master
all the intervals, you become a good sight
reader.

Chords

MAJOR AND MINOR TRIADS

The Major triad is a three note chord built
on the 1st, 3rd and 5th degrees of the Major scale. From the root, it may be thought
of as a Major 3rd and perfect 5th. The interval between the 3rd and 5th degrees is a
minor 3rd.

A minor triad is built on the 1st, 3rd and
5th degrees of the minor scale. From the
root, it may be thought of as a minor 3rd
and a perfect 5th. The interval between the
3rd and 5th degrees is a Major 3rd.

If the three notes of the triad are played
individually (C-E-G), we call it a "broken"
chord or "arpeggio". If the three notes of
the triad are sounded together, we call it
a "block" chord.

broken chord   block chord

Only a chordal instrument such as the piano
or guitar may play the three notes simul-
taneously. Obviously, one singer alone cannot sing a block chord. But when three
singers get together and each sing a note
of the triad, the result is "harmony".

1. Using the Major triad, sing:

  1-3-5-5-3-1
  1-5-3-1
  5-1-3-1
  5-1-3-5-1

2. Repeat using the minor triad.

3. Sing this melody:

THE DIMINISHED TRIAD

The diminished triad is a three note chord, consisting of the root, the minor 3rd and the diminished 5th. From the root, these are two consecutive minor 3rds. We call it 'diminished' because the relationship between the root and 5th is a diminished 5th interval.

    1. Sing:

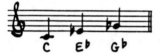

    2. Repeat the above with other starting notes.

THE AUGMENTED TRIAD

The augmented triad is a three note chord, consisting of the root, the Major 3rd and the augmented 5th. Up from the root, these are two consecutive Major 3rds. We call it 'augmented' because the relationship between the root and 5th is an augmented 5th interval.

    1. Sing:

    2. Repeat using other starting notes.

THE MAJOR SEVENTH CHORD

A Major seventh chord is a four note chord that consists of a Major triad plus a Major seventh (from the root).

C Maj 7

C - E - G - B

    1. Sing up and down the notes of the Major seventh chord. Then repeat with other starting notes.

    2. Sing this melody:

THE MINOR SEVENTH CHORD

A minor seventh chord is a four note chord that consists of a minor triad plus a minor seventh (from the root).

Cm 7

C - E♭ - G - B♭

    1. Sing: up and down the notes of the minor seventh chord. Then repeat with various starting notes.

    2. Sing this melody:

THE DOMINANT SEVENTH CHORD

The dominant seventh chord is a four note
chord, consisting of a Major triad with a
minor seventh added. It is called "dominant" because it is built on the fifth degree (dominant) of the scale. This chord is
special because it leads to the tonic triad
(resolves).

It is also used as a "pivot" chord, 'modu-
lating' to a new key.

   Sing this melody:

THE HALF-DIMINISHED SEVENTH CHORD

The half-diminished seventh chord is a four
note chord consisting of a diminished triad
plus a minor seventh up from the root of
the chord.

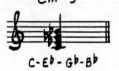

Sing up and down the four notes of the half-diminished seventh chord from various starting notes.

It will become easier as you work with these exer- cises to listen to a chord and pick out the root, 3rd, 5th or 7th. This ability is absolutely essential for many types of studio sing- ing and back-up.

METER - SIMPLE RHYTHMS

Every piece of music has a "meter" or a set timing that generally remains unaltered throughout. The piece is divided into "mea- sures" by "bar lines" which measure off the number of beats within each measure. The "Time signature" appears as a fraction, im- mediately following the G clef and key sig- nature. The top number indicates the number of beats within each measure. The number below indicates what kind of note equals one beat.

In 4/4 time, there are 4 beats to a measure and the quarter note gets 1 beat. In 6/8 time, there are six beats to a measure and the eighth note gets one beat.

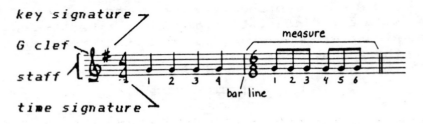

The most common time signatures are
4/4, 3/4, 2/4 and 6/8.

In 4/4 time, beats 1 and 3 are usually
accented, as in a march.

In 3/4 time, the accent falls on 1, as
in a waltz.

In 6/8 time, the accents fall on 1 and
4, which may have a waltz-like feel. But
at a faster tempo, it may be felt in 2.

In 4/4 time, the whole note and whole
rest hold for 4 beats.

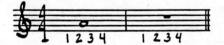

The half note and half rest hold for 2 beats.

The quarter note and quarter rest hold for 1 beat.

A beat is a unit of time which may be divided in half. The 'downbeat' begins the beat and the 'upbeat' begins the second half. (The first beat of each measure is commonly referred to as the downbeat.)

The eighth note and the eighth rest hold for 1/2 beat. You can feel the eighth note upbeat if you say the word "and" between the beats as you count (1 & 2 &....).

Sing:

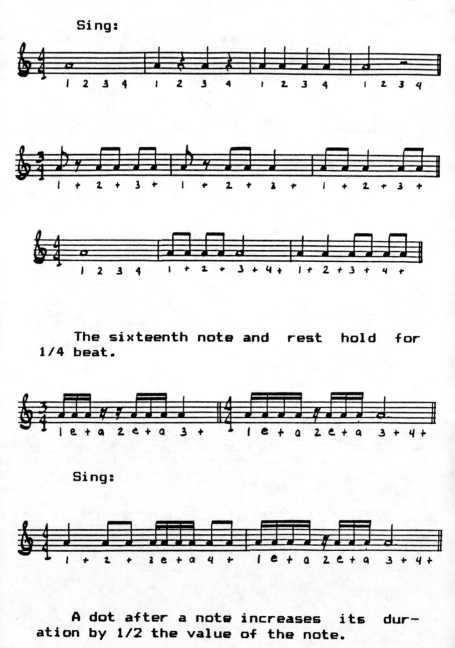

The sixteenth note and rest hold for 1/4 beat.

Sing:

A dot after a note increases its dur-ation by 1/2 the value of the note.

In 3/4 and 4/4 time, the dotted half note holds for 3 beats.

Sing:

The dotted quarter note is held for 1-1/2 beats and the dotted eighth for 3/4 beat.

Sing:

In 6/8 time, the eighth note and eighth rest hold for 1 beat.

The quarter note and quarter rest hold for 2 beats.

The dotted quarter note and dotted quarter rest hold for 3 beats.

The half note and half rest hold for 4 beats and the dotted half note holds for 6 beats.

Sing:

The TRIPLET is most commonly used in 4/4 and 3/4 meter. The eighth note triplet is a 3 note figure evenly dividing the duration of 1 beat.

The quarter note triplet is a 3 note figure evenly dividing the duration of 2 beats.

SYNCOPATION

Syncopation occurs whenever an accent is placed on an upbeat or on a 'weak' beat in a measure.

THE TIE

The tie is used to add note values of successive notes of the same pitch, indicating that they are sustained as one.

Sing:

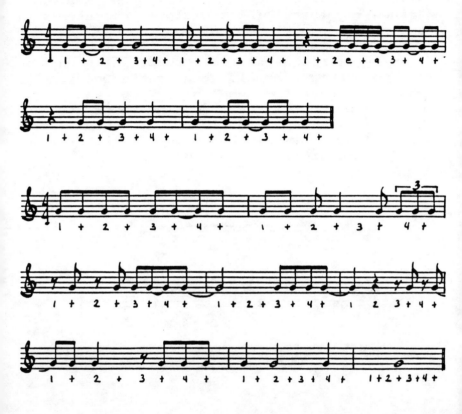

THE REPEAT SIGN

Repeat signs are used to indicate the repetition of the musical section between them.

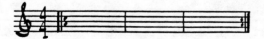

WORKING FROM SHEET MUSIC

The piano vocal score, commonly referred to
as "sheet music", consists of three staves
joined together. The top staff represents
the singer's part (melody and words). The
two lower staves (treble, bass), joined by
a bracket, represent the accompanist's part
(piano accompaniment). Vocal parts or har-
monies for baritone and bass are usually
written on the bass staff. The chord symbols usually appear just above the singer's
part. (Chord symbol charts are available in
most music stores.)

THE LEAD SHEET

...consists of the melody, words and chord
symbols. Rhythmic and/or melodic figures
are often added to assist the accompanist,
including 'riffs', 'fills', 'vamps', etc.
(see glossary, p. 120).

THE CHORD CHART

...consists of empty measures with the chord symbols indicated above them. Sometimes, key words of the lyric are added so that an accompanist can more easily follow the singer. Riffs, fills and/or vamps are often added as well.

Many Pop accompanists prefer to play from the chord symbols alone as they improvise their own "fills" or melodic lines around and between the vocal phrases of the singer. Classical accompanists play only the written notes of the score. Depending on the material, some musicians use a combination of these techniques.

An advantage in playing from the chord symbols is that transpositions to other keys or modulations (changes of key within the song) can be made more easily.

Very often, in Pop recording sessions and live shows, only a lead sheet or chord chart is available and the players must improvise using the chord symbols alone.

Singers´, be sure your musicians have appropriate charts.

TRANSPOSING A SONG

You may have to transpose a song (raise or lower the key) to accommodate your voice range. This means moving all the notes and chords (up or down) while retaining their original relationships. Such transpositions may be anywhere from a half step to a 5th. Most often, the key of the sheet music is chosen to suit the range of the average voice or for convenience of printing. Don't assume it to be the original key of the recording or score.

Learn how to 'shift' for yourself.
To find the best key:

    1.   If the song is too high, lower the key so that the highest notes of the song lie comfortably in your upper range. If the low notes are then too low, you may alter the melody where it is too low, making sure that your new melody is compatible with the chords.

    2.   If the song is too low, raise the key so that the highest notes of the song lie comfortably in your upper range.

    3.   If the song lies comfortably within your range, you may still want to transpose it. In general, a higher key will give your voice a brighter, more energetic sound; a lower key will give your voice a more mellow sound. Shifting the key even a half step up or down can make a significant difference.

You need only <u>write in the new chord symbols</u> directly above or beside and more prominent than the original chord symbols.

Use a dark <u>pencil</u>. Colored pencil could be difficult to read under the colored lights of a theater or night club. Don't use <u>ink</u> – you may change your mind. Write the chords boldly and legibly. Expect an accompanist to refuse to play from music that is illegible or has not been transposed. <u>Never</u> assume that your accompanist can transpose at sight.

<u>Do not fold</u> your music. Folded music has a way of <u>un</u>folding itself right <u>off</u> the music stand! This can create an embarrassing situation. Here again, musicians may refuse to play from music that cannot be set down in front of them without collapsing.

Be prepared! Be professional!

good luck and
keep singing!

* exercises *

Ex.1

A.	LOUD	SOFT	LOUD	~~~~~
B.	SOFT	LOUD	SOFT	~~~~~
C.	SOFT	MEDIUM	LOUD	~~~~~
D.	LOUD	MEDIUM	SOFT	~~~~~

Ex.2

A. LOUD / SOFT
B. LOUD / SOFT

Ex 3.

A. LOUD   SOFT
B. SOFT   LOUD
C. ——

Ex 4.

Ex 5.

A.
B.

* Practice *
* Words & Phrases *

This list proceeds from easiest to most difficult with regard to vowel and consonant combinations.

...on and on and...

...now and then and...

...why oh why oh...

...you and me and...

...day by day by...

...live and learn and...

...there and then and...

...slip and slide...

...come and stay and...

...tea for two for...

...stars and stripes and...

...sticks and stones and...

...scrape and scratch and...

...week to week to...

...chose and choose...

...storks and storms and...

* reading notes *

TREBLE CLEF
lines

A   MIDDLE C   E   G   B   D   F   A   HIGH C

spaces

G   B   D   F   A   C   E   G   B

BASS CLEF
lines

LOW C   E   G   B   D   F   A   MIDDLE C   E

spaces

D   F   A   C   E   G   B   D

—— Major ——

SHARPED KEYS
(circle of 5ths)

-- Major --

FLATTED KEYS
(circle of 4ths)

Glossary:
Musical Terms

A cappella: sung without accompaniment

A tempo: return to original or normal tempo after a departure (i.e. rit., ad lib, etc.)

Accel. (accelerando): gradually becoming faster

Ad lib. (ad libitum): freedom to vary from strict tempo

Adagio: slow tempo, between andante and largo

Al fine: to the end

Al segno: to the sign

Allargando: growing gradually slower

Allegro: quick tempo, lively

Aria: a cohesive section of music (song) for solo voice, within a larger work in classical style

Andante: moderately slow

Break (instrumental): instrumental interlude within a song

Cadence: a section of music, ending a composition.

Cadenza: an extended vocal section in free improvisatory style, usually at the end of an aria

Coda (⊕): an added section of music concluding the piece

Colla voce: accompaniment is to follow singers tempo

Cresc. (————,crescendo): growing gradually louder

Cue: musical, verbal or visual communication between singer and musicians

D.C. (da capo): ('from the top') from the beginning of the music

D.S. (dal segno): sing the section of music preceded by the sign,(𝄋)

Decresc. (————,decrescendo): gradually decreasing volume

Dim. (diminuendo): same as decrescendo

(⌒) Fermata: a suspension of tempo on a sustained note or on a rest

Fill: melody played by an accompanying instrument in between the phrases of singing

Fine: end

Forte (f):   loud

Fortissimo (ff): very loud

Gliss. (ᵐᵐ or ᵐᵐ ,glissando): sliding from one pitch to another

Hook: memorable, 'catchy' musical and/or verbal phrase

Intro (introduction): opening accompaniment leading to the entrance of the singer

Largo: very slow

Legato: smoothly and connected

Lent, Lento: slowly

Lick: a melodic embellishment on a syllable or word, usually improvised

Meno: less

Mezzo forte (mf):   moderately loud

Mezzo piano (mp):   moderately soft

Molto: very (e.g., molto allegro — very fast)

Non troppo: not too much (e.g., non troppo allegro — not too fast)

Pianissimo (pp):   very soft

Piano (p):   soft

Piu: more (e.g., piu forte — louder)

Poco: little (e.g., poco allegro — a little faster)

Poco a poco: little by little

Presto: very fast

Railroad Tracks (//):   complete (silent) pause in the music

Rall. (rallentando):   gradually slowing down

Riff: a repeating melodic or rhythmic figure

Rit. (Ritard, Ritardando):   same as rallentando

Rubato: flexibility and freedom of tempo

Sforzando (*sf, sfz*): strong accent on a single note or chord

Sostenuto: momentarily slackening the tempo

Staccato: detached and short note, indicated by a dot above the note, a reduction of its written duration by half or more

Subito: sudden, immediate (e.g., subito piano — suddenly soft)

Tacet: be silent

Tag: a short added ending

Tenuto: sustain

Tessitura: the general range in which the majority of notes lie in a song, aria, etc.

Vamp: repeating musical pattern of flexible duration, used as an intro to a song, between verses or exit music

Vivace: fast and lively

Vocal Terms

PREPARATION: a state of readiness to sing, the moment before the sound is produced — a full breath has been taken, throat and resonators are open, support is created (preparation should occur with each breath)

SUPPORT: a co-ordination for precision control of air pressure, a 'dynamic tension' between the muscles of inhaling and the muscles of exhaling

FOCUSING: approximating the vocal cords, controlling breathiness, clarity and volume

PLACEMENT: the art of coloring the vocal tone, using the resonators — head, nasal, mouth, chest

RESONANCE: refers to the way in which the resonators contribute to the 'quality' (color) of the vocal sound

FORWARD PLACEMENT, MASK or FRONTAL RESONANCE: having nasal/mouth resonance, created by an unobstructed channel for the vocal tone

DIAPHRAGMATIC/ABDOMINAL: referring to a large configuration of muscles in the body's mid-section capable of precision control of air flow (for support, vibrato, volume, etc.)

VIBRATO: a wave-like pulse in the sustained tone — when produced diaphragmatically, can be controlled for speed, depth, smoothness

REGISTERS: upper and lower parts of a
vocal range, usually differing in quality
and overlapping

THE BREAK: an abrupt change in vocal
quality when moving from one register to
the other

HEAD VOICE = UPPER REGISTER = FALSETTO =
SOPRANO VOICE

CHEST VOICE = LOWER REGISTER = SPEAKING
RANGE = ALTO = 'BELT'

UPPER MIX: the sound the upper register
can produce to imitate and match the lower
register; used as an upward extension of
the lower register sound

LOWER MIX: the sound the lower register
can produce to imitate and match the upper
register classical quality; used as an
dowward extension of the upper register.

MIXED REGISTER/MIXING: moving freely
between upper and lower registers with a
smooth and matching vocal quality

Available From VOCAL POWER INSTITUTE

BORN TO SING BY Elisabeth Howard/Howard Austin

VOCAL TECHNIQUE COURSE (BTS-T) (Book with Tape)
Complete Course in Basic Techniques **$19.95**
Technique Book only ....(Book T) - $12.95
Technique Tape only ....(Tape T) - $12.95

VOCAL STYLE COURSE (BTS-S) (Book with Tape)
STYLE and personal style **$19.95**
Style book alone ....(Book S) - $12.95
Style tape alone ....(Tape S) - $12.95

VOCAL HARMONY COURSE (BTS-H) (Book with Tape) -
Reading music, Ear Training, Harmonizing.......**$19.95**
Harmony Book alone ....(Book H) - $12.95
Harmony Tape alone ....(Tape H) - $12.95

All three courses: Technique, Style and Harmony
(# VPC-4) (3 books and 3 Tapes) **$44.95**

WARM-UP / WORKOUT Exercises and Basic Ear
Training.................................(Tape 4) - $12.95

ADVANCED VOCAL TECHNIQUE..(Tape T2) - $12.95

BORN TO SING Book (BTS-0): Technique, Style,
Musicianship......................................$12.95

BORN TO SING Starter Set ......(Tapes T & S) - $19.95

BORN TO SING Deluxe (Book-0 plus Tapes T, T2, S)
(VPC-3N)...**$39.95**

INSTRUCTOR'S GUIDE Book of Teaching Methods,
Lesson Plans, etc. - *use with VPC-3N*.........$12.95

VPC-3 with Guide (VPC-E) $49.95

* Born To Sing VIDEO (BTS-VT)
Complete Basic Course in Vocal Technique...$29.95 ☐

BORN TO SING - LESSONS BY MAIL (ON TAPE) ...
FREE INFORMATION BROCHURE ....

POWER SPEECH by Geoffrey G. Forward

*** With EXPLANATIONS, DEMONSTRATIONS, EXERCISES ***

SPEECH BASICS Relaxation, Breathing, Support,
Resonance, Projection, Diction, Emphasis,
Intonation/Inflection, Power, Stamina, Speech
Awareness Training.....................(2 Tapes) - $24.95

DAILY WORKOUT EXERCISES ....(1 Tape) - $9.95

OVER

SINGER'S GUIDE by Wayland Pickard

==================

Complete **SINGER'S GUIDE** to becoming a working professional - Includes everything from How to write your own charts to How to promote and market your talent. . . find your vocal range. . . communicate with & conduct the band. . . choose songs. . . musical equipment. . create a great demo. . . get bookings.

Singer's Guide provides what you need to know about - auditioning. . .showcasing. . .touring. . .charts. . .styles. . . music language. . . and more. . .

200 page book $24.95

==================

LIFE LINE by Howard Austin

==================

LIFE LINE Relaxation Tape - A relaxed mind and body releases the creative spirit. This Deeply Soothing Recording Will Refresh You, Stir Your Creative Energy And Enhance The Quality Of Your Sleep $9.95
